Unit
Assessments

D1558488

Mc
Graw
Hill

mheducation.com/prek-12

Send all inquiries to:
McGraw-Hill Education
Two Penn Plaza
New York, New York 10121

ISBN: 978-0-07-901757-4
MHID: 0-07-901757-6

Printed in the United States of America.

2 3 4 5 6 7 8 9 QVS 24 23 22 21 20 19   B

Table of Contents

Unit Assessments

The *Unit Assessments* component is an integral part of the complete assessment program aligned with *Wonders* and state standards.

Purpose

This component reports on the outcome of student learning. As students complete each unit of the reading program, they will be assessed on their understanding of key instructional content and their ability to write to source texts/stimuli. The results serve as a summative assessment by providing a status of current achievement in relation to student progress through the curriculum. The results of the assessments can be used to inform subsequent instruction, aid in making leveling and grouping decisions, and point toward areas in need of reteaching or remediation.

Focus

Unit Assessments focuses on key areas of English Language Arts—comprehension of literature and informational text, vocabulary acquisition and use, command of the conventions of the English language, and genre writing in response to sources.

Each unit assessment also provides students familiarity with the item types, the test approaches, and the increased rigor associated with the advances in state-mandated high-stakes assessments.

Test Administration

Each unit assessment should be administered once the instruction for the specific unit is completed. Make copies of the unit assessment for the class. You will need copies of the answer key pages that feature the scoring charts for each student taking the assessment, which provide a place to list student scores. The data from each unit assessment charts student progress and underscores strengths and weaknesses.

This component is the pencil-and-paper version of the assessment. You can administer the online version of the test, which allows for technology-enhanced item functionality.

NOTE: Due to time constraints, you may wish to administer the unit assessment over multiple days. For example, students can complete the 25-item test on the first day and complete the performance task on another. For planning purposes, the recommended time for each performance task is 90–100 minutes over two back-to-back sessions. During the first session, provide students 30–40 minutes to read the stimulus materials and answer the research questions. During the second session, provide students 60–70 minutes for planning, writing, and editing their responses. If desired, provide students a short break between sessions. If you decide to break-up administration by assessment sections, please remember to withhold those sections of the test students are not completing to ensure test validity.

After each student has a copy of the assessment, provide a version of the following directions:

Teacher Introduction

Say: *Write your name on the question pages for this assessment.* (When students are finished, continue with the directions.) *You will read three texts and answer questions about them. In the next part of the test, you will read a student draft that you will revise or edit for the correct grammar, mechanics, and usage. In the final part of the test, you will read sources, answer questions about them, and write a response based on the assignment you will find, which will ask you to use those sources in your writing.*

Read each part of the test carefully. For multiple-choice questions, circle the letter next to the correct answer or answers. For other types of questions, look carefully at the directions. You may be asked to match items, circle or underline choices, or complete a chart. For the constructed-response question, write your response on the lines provided. For the performance task, write your response to the assignment on separate sheets of paper. When you have completed the assessment, put your pencil down and turn the pages over. You may begin now.

Answer procedural questions during the assessment, but do not provide any assistance on the items or selections. Have extra paper on hand for students to use for their performance task responses. After the class has completed the assessment, ask students to verify that their names are written on the necessary pages.

Assessment Items

Unit assessments feature the following item types—selected response (SR), multiple selected response (MSR), evidence-based selected response (EBSR), constructed response (CR), and technology-enhanced items (TE). (Please note that the print versions of TE items are available in this component; the full functionality of the items is available only through the online assessment.) This variety of item types provides multiple methods of assessing student understanding, allows for deeper investigation into skills and strategies, and provides students an opportunity to become familiar with the kinds of questions they will encounter in state-mandated summative assessments.

Performance Tasks

Each unit features a performance task (PT) assessment in a previously taught genre.
The task types are:

- Narrative
  - Students craft a narrative using information from the sources.

- Informational
  - Students generate a thesis based on the sources and use information from the sources to explain this thesis.

- Opinion
  - Students analyze the ideas in sources and make a claim that they support using the sources.

Each PT assesses standards that address comprehension, research skills, genre writing, and the use of standard English language conventions (ELC). The stimulus texts and research questions in each task build toward the goal of the final writing topic.

Teacher Introduction

Overview

- Students will read three texts in each assessment and respond to items focusing on comprehension skills, literary elements, text features, and vocabulary strategies. These items assess the ability to access meaning from the text and demonstrate understanding of unknown and multiple-meaning words and phrases.

- Students will then read a student draft that requires corrections or clarifications to its use of the conventions of standard English language or complete a cloze passage that requires correct usage identification.

- Students are then presented with a performance task assessment.

Each test item in *Unit Assessments* (as well as in progress monitoring and benchmark assessments) has a Depth of Knowledge (DOK) level assigned to it.

Vocabulary items

DOK 1: Use word parts (affixes, roots) to determine the meaning of an unknown word.

DOK 2: Use context or print/digital resources to determine the meaning of an unknown or multiple-meaning word; use context to understand figurative language.

Comprehension items

DOK 1: Identify/locate information in the text.

DOK 2: Analyze text structures/literary elements.

DOK 3: Make inferences using text evidence and analyze author's craft.

DOK 4: Respond using multiple texts.

Revising and Editing items

DOK 1: Edit to fix errors

DOK 2: Revise for clarity and coherence.

Each unit assessment features three "cold reads" on which the comprehension and vocabulary assessment items are based. These selections reflect the unit theme and genre-studies to support the focus of the classroom instruction. Texts fall within the Lexile band 420L-650L. Complexity on this quantitative measure grows throughout the units, unless a qualitative measure supports text placement outside a lockstep Lexile continuum.

Comprehension

Comprehension items assess student understanding of the text through the use of the comprehension skills, literary elements, and text features taught throughout the unit.

Teacher Introduction

Vocabulary

Vocabulary items ask students to demonstrate their ability to uncover the meanings of unknown and multiple-meaning words and phrases using vocabulary strategies.

English Language Conventions/Phonics

Ten items in each unit ask students to demonstrate their command of the conventions of standard English and phonics.

Performance Task

Students complete one performance task per unit, which includes research questions and a final written response in the specified task genre.

Scoring

Each unit assessment totals 40 points. Comprehension and vocabulary items are worth two points each. Constructed-response and multi-part items should be answered correctly in full, though you may choose to provide partial credit. English language conventions and phonics items are worth one point each. Use the scoring chart at the bottom of the answer key to record each student's score. Note that the performance task is scored separately, as described below.

For the constructed-response items, assign a score using the correct response parameters provided in the answer key along with the scoring rubrics shown below. Responses that show a complete lack of understanding or are left blank should be given a *0*.

Short Response Score 2: The response is well-crafted and concise and shows a thorough understanding of the underlying skill. Appropriate text evidence is used to answer the question.

Short Response Score 1: The response shows partial understanding of the underlying skill. Text evidence is featured, though examples are too general.

Each unit performance task is a separate 15-point assessment. The three research items are worth a total of five points, broken down as indicated in the scoring charts. Score the written response holistically on a 10-point scale, using the rubrics on the following pages:

- 4 points for purpose/organization [P/O]

- 4 points for evidence/elaboration [E/E] or development/elaboration [D/E]

- 2 points for English language conventions [C]

- Unscorable or 0-point responses are unrelated to the topic, illegible, contain little or no writing, or show little to no command of the conventions of standard English.

Use the top-score anchor paper response provided in the answer key for each test for additional scoring guidance.

Teacher Introduction

NARRATIVE PERFORMANCE TASK SCORING RUBRIC

Score	Purpose/Organization	Development/Elaboration	Conventions
4	• **fully sustained** organization; **clear** focus • effective, unified plot • effective development of setting, characters, point of view • transitions clarify relationships between and among ideas • logical sequence of events • effective opening and closing	• **effective** elaboration with details, dialogue, description • clear expression of experiences and events • effective use of relevant source material • effective use of various narrative techniques • effective use of sensory, concrete, and figurative language	
3	• **adequately sustained** organization; **generally maintained** focus • evident plot with loose connections • adequate development of setting, characters, point of view • adequate use of transitional strategies • adequate sequence of events • adequate opening and closing	• **adequate** elaboration with details, dialogue, description • adequate expression of experiences and events • adequate use of source material • adequate use of various narrative techniques • adequate use of sensory, concrete, and figurative language	
2	• **somewhat sustained** organization; **uneven** focus • inconsistent plot with evident flaws • uneven development of setting, characters, point of view • uneven use of transitional strategies, with little variety • weak or uneven sequence of events • weak opening and closing	• **uneven** elaboration with **partial** details, dialogue, description • uneven expression of experiences and events • vague, abrupt, or imprecise use of source material • uneven, inconsistent use of narrative technique • partial or weak use of sensory, concrete, and figurative language	• **adequate** command of spelling, capitalization, punctuation, grammar, and usage • few errors
1	• **basic** organization; **little or no** focus • little or no discernible plot; may just be a series of events • brief or no development of setting, characters, point of view • few or no transitional strategies • little or no organization of event sequence; extraneous ideas • no opening and/or closing	• **minimal** elaboration with **few or no** details, dialogue, description • confusing expression of experiences and events • little or no use of source material • minimal or incorrect use of narrative techniques • little or no use of sensory, concrete, and figurative language	• **partial** command of spelling, capitalization, punctuation, grammar, and usage • some patterns of errors

Teacher Introduction

INFORMATIONAL PERFORMANCE TASK SCORING RUBRIC

Score	Purpose/Organization	Evidence/Elaboration	Conventions
4	• **effective** organizational structure • clear statement of main idea based on purpose, audience, task • consistent use of various transitions • logical progression of ideas	• **convincing** support for main idea; **effective** use of sources • integrates comprehensive evidence from sources • relevant references • effective use of elaboration • audience-appropriate domain-specific vocabulary	
3	• **evident** organizational structure • adequate statement of main idea based on purpose, audience, task • adequate, somewhat varied use of transitions • adequate progression of ideas	• **adequate** support for main idea; **adequate** use of sources • some integration of evidence from sources • references may be general • adequate use of some elaboration • generally audience-appropriate domain-specific vocabulary	
2	• **inconsistent** organizational structure • unclear or somewhat unfocused main idea • inconsistent use of transitions with little variety • formulaic or uneven progression of ideas	• **uneven** support for main idea; **limited** use of sources • weakly integrated, vague, or imprecise evidence from sources • references are vague or absent • weak or uneven elaboration • uneven domain-specific vocabulary	• **adequate** command of spelling, capitalization, punctuation, grammar, and usage • few errors
1	• **little or no** organizational structure • few or no transitions • frequent extraneous ideas; may be formulaic • may lack introduction and/or conclusion • confusing or ambiguous focus; may be very brief	• **minimal** support for main idea; **little or no** use of sources • minimal, absent, incorrect, or irrelevant evidence from sources • references are absent or incorrect • minimal, if any, elaboration • limited or ineffective domain-specific vocabulary	• **partial** command of spelling, capitalization, punctuation, grammar, and usage • some patterns of errors

Teacher Introduction

OPINION PERFORMANCE TASK SCORING RUBRIC

Score	Purpose/Organization	Evidence/Elaboration	Conventions
4	• **effective** organizational structure; **sustained** focus • consistent use of various transitions • logical progression of ideas • effective introduction and conclusion • clearly communicated opinion for purpose, audience, task	• **convincing** support/evidence for main idea; **effective** use of sources; **precise** language • comprehensive evidence from sources is integrated • relevant, specific references • effective elaborative techniques • appropriate domain-specific vocabulary for audience, purpose	
3	• **evident** organizational structure; **adequate** focus • adequate use of transitions • adequate progression of ideas • adequate introduction and conclusion • clear opinion, mostly maintained, though loosely • adequate opinion for purpose, audience, task	• **adequate** support/evidence for main idea; **adequate** use of sources; **general** language • some evidence from sources is integrated • general, imprecise references • adequate elaboration • generally appropriate domain-specific vocabulary for audience, purpose	
2	• **inconsistent** organizational structure; **somewhat sustained** focus • inconsistent use of transitions • uneven progression of ideas • introduction or conclusion, if present, may be weak • somewhat unclear or unfocused opinion	• **uneven** support for main idea; **partial** use of sources; **simple** language • evidence from sources is weakly integrated, vague, or imprecise • vague, unclear references • weak or uneven elaboration • uneven or somewhat ineffective use of domain-specific vocabulary for audience, purpose	• **adequate** command of spelling, capitalization, punctuation, grammar, and usage • few errors
1	• **little or no** organizational structure or focus • few or no transitions • frequent extraneous ideas are evident; may be formulaic • introduction and/or conclusion may be missing • confusing opinion	• **minimal** support for main idea; **little or no** use of sources; **vague** language • source material evidence is minimal, incorrect, or irrelevant • references absent or incorrect • minimal, if any, elaboration • limited or ineffective use of domain-specific vocabulary for audience, purpose	• **partial** command of spelling, capitalization, punctuation, grammar, and usage • some patterns of errors

Evaluating Scores

The answer keys have been constructed to provide the information you need to aid your understanding of student performance, as well as individualized instructional and intervention needs.

This column lists the instructional content from the unit that is assessed in each item.

Question	Correct Answer	Content Focus	Complexity

This column lists the Depth of Knowledge associated with each item.

MSR item

Question	Correct Answer	Content Focus	Complexity
6	A, C	Context Clues: Synonyms	DOK 2
7A	C	Main Idea and Key Details	DOK 2
7B	D	Main Idea and Key Details/Text Evidence	DOK 2

Although text evidence is a key component in all items, it is called out explicitly in EBSR items.

Comprehension: 1, 2A, 2B, 4, 7A, 7B, 8, 9, 11, 12A, 12B, 15	/18	%
Vocabulary 3, 5, 6, 10, 13, 14	/12	%
English Language Conventions 16, 17, 18, 19, 20	/5	%
Phonics 21, 22, 23, 24, 25	/5	%
Total Unit 1 Assessment Score	/40	%

Scoring rows identify items associated with the assessed skills and allow for quick record keeping.

Teacher Introduction

Narrative Performance Task			
Question	**Answer**	**Complexity**	**Score**
1	see below	DOK 2	/1
2	see below	DOK 3	/2
3	see below	DOK 3	/2
Story	see below	DOK 4	/4 [P/O] /4 [D/E] /2 [C]
Total Score			**/15**

> This scoring row identifies the elements of the holistic scoring rubric.

The goal of each unit assessment is to evaluate student mastery of previously-taught material.

The expectation is for students to score 80% or higher on the unit assessment as a whole; within this score, the expectation is for students to score 75% or higher on each section of the assessment. For the performance task, the expectation also is for students to score 80% or higher, or 12 or higher on the entire task, and 8 or higher on the written response.

For students who do not meet these benchmarks, assign appropriate lessons from the relevant **Tier 2 online PDFs**. Refer to the unit assessment pages in the Teacher's Edition of *Wonders* for specific lessons. For the performance task, the expectation is for students to score 12 or higher on the entire task, and 8 or higher on the written response.

Read the passage. Then answer the questions.

Do-It-Yourself Dinner

A new family moved in next door to Rico. Rico's mama asked them to come to dinner on Friday. Rico was happy about this. He wanted to meet the new neighbors.

Mama was very busy all week. Now it was Friday morning. "I have no idea what to cook," she said.

"We can have a do-it-yourself dinner," Rico said. "We can have tacos. We can make our own."

"That is a good idea, but it will still take work. We will have to pick what to buy from the store."

Rico got a pencil and paper. He made a list: taco shells, lettuce, cheese, and meat.

Mama added, "Do not forget beans, onions, and tomatoes."

That afternoon, Mama picked Rico up after school. They went to the store. The parking lot was very full.

"Look at all of the cars!" Mama said. "This could take a long time."

"I have an idea," Rico said. "Let's cut the list in two. I can get half, and you can get the other half."

GO ON →

Inside the store, Rico and Mama each got a shopping basket. Rico found the tomatoes, onions, lettuce, and cheese. Mama headed to the back of the store to get the meat, beans, and taco shells. They met at the front of the store. Mama paid for the food.

Soon, Mama and Rico were driving home. A bag full of food sat on the back seat.

At home Rico said, "I can wash tomatoes." He hurried into the kitchen.

Rico and Mama worked fast. They helped each other. They were almost done. Then Mama said, "Oh, no! We still have to set the kitchen table!"

"I can do it," said Rico. He put out plates and glasses. Then he heard the doorbell. Rico opened the door. He said, "Hello! We're having a do-it-yourself dinner."

GO ON →

The new neighbors and their daughter, Ella, came in. Everyone sat at the table. They each took a taco shell. They passed plates of lettuce, onions, and tomatoes. They passed bowls of meat, beans, and cheese. They passed a jar of hot sauce. They each took what they wanted. Each built a perfect taco. Ella did not want meat. She piled more beans on her taco. Rico loved spicy food. He put lots of hot sauce on his taco.

Everyone smiled and laughed as Mama and Rico learned about their friendly neighbors. At last, everyone was full.

Ella said, "We all made our own tacos. Now, we can all wash and dry the dishes." Everyone agreed. Soon, the kitchen was filled with the sound of laughter as the new friends worked together to clean up.

"This has been so much fun," the new neighbors said. "We will have a do-it-yourself dinner next week. Come to our house. We'll make little pizzas. We can each make our own pizza!"

GO ON →

1   The following question has two parts. First, answer part A.
    Then, answer part B.

    Part A: How does the reader know that Rico's mama
    is kind?

    A She works very hard.

    B She lets Rico cook alone.

    C She drives Rico to the store.

    D She welcomes new neighbors.

    Part B: Which sentence from the passage **best** helps you
    answer part A?

    A A new family moved in next door to Rico.

    B Rico's mama asked them to come to dinner on Friday.

    C "That is a good idea, but it will still take work."

    D "Oh, no! We still have to set the kitchen table!"

2   Why is Mama worried about Friday's dinner?

    A Mama does not know who is coming to eat.

    B Mama is not very good at cooking.

    C Mama is too busy all week to get anything ready.

    D Mama wants to do something else that night.

GO ON →

3   What does the picture in the passage show about Rico? Pick **two** choices.

    A   He enjoys eating tacos.

    B   He wants to make new friends.

    C   He helps clean the food.

    D   He works in the kitchen.

    E   He writes a shopping list.

4   Read the sentence from the passage.

Mama <u>added</u>, "Do not forget beans, onions, and tomatoes."

Pick **two** words that have the same root word as <u>added</u>. Draw a circle around each one.

adding

address

adds

admit

adventure

GO ON →

5 Why does Rico suggest that Mama and he cut the shopping list in half?

    A So they can finish more quickly.

    B So they can buy more food items.

    C So they can race to finish first.

    D So they can carry fewer bags of food.

6 Complete the chart with the places from the setting of "Do-It-Yourself Dinner." Mark an X in the box to show **one** setting for **each** part of the story. Not all places will be used. A place may be used more than once.

	Rico's home	Ella's home	the store
Beginning of story	☐	☐	☐
Middle of story	☐	☐	☐
End of story	☐	☐	☐

GO ON →

Read the passage. Then answer the questions.

Jam Day

It is early in the morning. Rabbit has been up for a long time. He is very excited. For Rabbit, this is just about the best day of the year. His family is going to a big farm way out in the country. They are going to pick blackberries. Rabbit loves to pick berries and make jam. Rabbit's mom and dad call it Jam Day.

Rabbit's family has Jam Day every year. First, everyone picks blackberries. Then, they take the berries home to their house. Rabbit helps his mom make enough jam to last all year. They work for hours to make the jam.

The jam tastes great. Rabbit and his parents eat it on bread. They eat it on leaves. They even eat it on bark. Sometimes Rabbit dips a spoon into the jam jar. Then he eats the jam by itself.

Rabbit's friends like to eat the jam, too. They like to come over to play. Rabbit's mom always has jam. Rabbit's friends eat jam with bread, leaves, and bark. The friend who likes the jam best is Chipmunk. Chipmunk comes to Rabbit's house almost every day to eat jam.

This year Chipmunk is picking blackberries, too. Chipmunk will come with Rabbit's family. It will be Chipmunk's first Jam Day. They drive to the farm. Rabbit's parents bring a lot of pails. They will fill all of them with ripe berries.

GO ON →

The day is sunny and warm. The bushes are full of blackberries. Rabbit and Chipmunk start picking right away. Each has a pail. Rabbit shows Chipmunk which are the best berries to pick. He shows him how to get berries without getting stuck by thorns. When they fill their pails, they put them by the car. Then they get empty pails. They pick and pick.

Chipmunk picks blackberries very fast. Rabbit is surprised. He remembers that it took him a long time to learn.

Later, there are many pails of blackberries. All the pails are full. Rabbit goes over to his dad. "Look at all the blackberries Chipmunk picked, Dad. This is his first Jam Day. But he filled just as many pails as you."

Rabbit's dad is silent for a minute. "You are right, Rabbit. Chipmunk has done a great job. How did you learn to pick blackberries so fast, Chipmunk?"

Chipmunk replied, "I worked very hard. I tried to make up for all the jam I have eaten at your house!"

GO ON →

7 Read the sentence from the passage.

Rabbit helps his mom make enough jam to <u>last</u> all year.

Which word means the same as the word <u>last</u>?

A keep

B next

C end

D quit

8 Read the sentences from the passage.

"Look at all the blackberries Chipmunk picked, Dad. This is his first Jam Day. But he filled just as many pails as you."

Which **two** words from the sentences have an ending that means something happened in the past?

A look

B picked

C first

D filled

E many

GO ON →

9 The following question has two parts. First, answer part A. Then, answer part B.

Part A: What surprises Rabbit on Jam Day?

A Rabbit's mom makes jam.

B The jam lasts all year.

C Chipmunk can pick blackberries fast.

D Rabbit's dad is silent for a minute.

Part B: Which sentence from the passage **best** helps you answer part A?

A They work for hours to make the jam.

B Sometimes Rabbit dips a spoon into the jam jar.

C "How did you learn to pick blackberries so fast, Chipmunk?"

D "Look at all the blackberries Chipmunk picked, Dad."

GO ON →

10 How can you tell that Chipmunk likes to eat jam? Use **two** details from the passage in your answer.

_____

_____

_____

_____

_____

11 Read the sentence from the passage.

Rabbit's dad is <u>silent</u> for a minute.

Which **two** words have almost the same meaning as <u>silent</u>?

A loud

B still

C upset

D quiet

E happy

GO ON →

Read the passage. Then answer the questions.

Big Babies!

We use the word <u>tiny</u> to tell about human babies. However, some babies are not tiny. Animals such as elephants and hippos have very large babies.

Elephant Babies

A baby elephant weighs 200 pounds. It is born hairy, but it loses its hair as it is growing. It will grow to be much bigger than 200 pounds.

A baby elephant drinks its mother's milk. It can do this until it is ten years old!

Baby elephants have to learn how to stand up. Next, they learn how to use their trunks. They learn how to lift and carry things with their trunks.

Young elephants like to play. They chase each other. They climb on each other. They throw sticks in the air with their trunks. They also use their trunks to be friendly. They wrap their trunks around each other. That is an elephant hug!

Elephants live in groups called herds. The elephants in a herd help keep each other safe. The mothers live in one herd. The fathers live in another. Babies live with their mothers. The grandmothers and aunts help take care of the babies.

GO ON →

Animal Birth Weights

Animal	Weight When Born
elephant	200 pounds
giraffe	150 pounds
hippo	100 pounds
zebra	65 pounds

Baby Hippos

Hippo babies weigh 100 pounds. They are born knowing how to swim. Some hippos are born on land. Many are born in water.

A baby hippo drinks its mother's milk. This is its food for about eight months. It can drink under the water. The baby closes its ears and nose so water will not come in while it is drinking milk.

A mother hippo stays in the water with her new baby for a few days. She does not even eat. She waits until the baby is ready. Then she takes it out of the water. She takes it with her to find food.

The father hippo also helps take care of the baby. He keeps it safe. Lions and other animals want to eat it! So the father hippo stands at the edge of the water. The mother and baby stay toward the middle of the water. Lions cannot get past the father hippo. The baby stays safe.

GO ON →

The mother hippo stays very close to the baby. She helps keep it safe, too. The mother and father hippos work together. They take good care of their baby.

Hippos live in groups of families. These groups are called schools. Father and mother hippos live together in the same school with other families. The families help each other. When a baby hippo's mother and father are busy, another hippo in the school takes care of the baby.

GO ON →

12   Read the sentence from the passage.

We use the word <u>tiny</u> to tell about human babies.

Which word has almost the same meaning as <u>tiny</u>?

A alone

B safe

C small

D under

13   What does the chart in the passage show readers?

A Elephant babies are larger than many other animal babies.

B Hippo babies are taller than elephant babies when born.

C Some animals have more than one baby at a time.

D Small animals often have large babies.

GO ON →

14   Fill in each empty box of the chart below with the correct root word, inflectional ending, or new word.

Root Word	Ending	New Word
grow	ing	
call		called
	ing	drinking

15   Which idea from the passage is shown in the picture?

A   A baby hippo stays with its mother.

B   A mother hippo gets helps from other hippos.

C   A mother hippo gives its baby milk.

D   A baby hippo can drink under the water.

GO ON →

The draft below needs revision. Read the draft. Then answer the questions.

Breakfast in Bed

(1) Mike does not know what to give his mom for her birthday. (2) his dad tries to help, telling Mike to make a gift. (3) But Mike says, "I did that last year."

(4) Then Dad says, You can make Mom breakfast in bed. (5) I will help you!" (6) Mike loves the idea. (7) He wants to make pancakes.

(8) Now it is Mom's birthday. (9) Mike is in the kitchen. (10) Dad is in the kitchen. (11) Dad has everything ready.

(12) Mike helps Dad stir the bowl. (13) Dad pours neat yellow circles. (14) Dad flips the pancakes. (15) He even lets Mike flip one!

(16) They put the pancakes on a tray and bring the tray to Mom. (17) Mom is happy. (18) She takes a bite of her pancakes. (19) She says, "These are the best birthday pancakes ever."

GO ON →

16 What is the **best** way to write sentence 2?

  A His dad tries to help, telling Mike to make a gift.

  B his dad tries to help, telling Mike, to make a gift.

  C his dad tries to help, telling mike to make a gift.

  D his dad tries to help, telling Mike to make a gift?

17 What is the correct way to write sentences 4 and 5?

  A Then Dad says, You can make Mom breakfast in bed.
  I will help you!

  B Then Dad says, "You can make Mom breakfast in bed.
  I will help you!"

  C Then "Dad says, You can make Mom breakfast in bed.
  I will help you!"

  D Then Dad says, "You can make Mom breakfast in bed."
  I will help you!

18 What is the **best** way to combine sentences 9 and 10?

  A Mike is in the kitchen, and Dad is in the kitchen.

  B Mike but Dad are in the kitchen.

  C Mike and Dad are in the kitchen.

  D Mike is in the kitchen, but Dad is in the kitchen.

GO ON →

19 Read this new detail.

The pancakes bubble first.

What is the **best** way to add this detail to sentence 14?

A The pancakes bubble because Dad flips them.

B Dad flips the pancakes to make them bubble.

C Dad flips the pancakes, and then they bubble.

D The pancakes bubble, and then Dad flips them.

20 What is the correct way to write sentence 19?

A She says "These are the best birthday pancakes ever."

B She says, "These are the best Birthday pancakes ever."

C She says, "These are the best birthday pancakes ever!"

D She says, "These are the best birthday pancakes ever.

GO ON →

Student Name _____

Answer these questions.

21 Which word has the short <u>a</u> sound?

    A cake

    B tap

    C tape

22 Which word has the short <u>e</u> sound?

    A bean

    B bee

    C beg

23 Which word has the same two-letter blend as <u>trip</u>?

    A rim

    B tip

    C tree

GO ON →

24 Which word has the same long <u>a</u> vowel sound as <u>made</u>?

    A bad

    B name

    C mad

25 Which word has the same long <u>i</u> vowel sound as <u>pine</u>?

    A it

    B pin

    C time

Narrative Performance Task

Task:

Your class has been learning about how families and friends learn, grow, and help one another. Now your class is going to make a class book to share what they have learned. Each student will write something for the book.

Before you decide what you will write about, you will read two passages, or sources, that provide information about how people and animals help each other. After you have looked at these passages, or sources, you will answer some questions about them. Look at the passages and the three questions that follow. Then, go back and read the passages carefully. They will give you the information you will need to answer the questions and write a narrative, or story, for the class book.

In Part 2, you will write your story using information from the two passages.

Directions for Part 1

You will now look at two passages, or sources. You can look at either of the passages as often as you like.

Research Questions:

After looking at the passages, use the rest of the time in Part 1 to answer three questions about them. Your answers to these questions will be scored. Also, your answers will help you think about the information you have read, which should help you write your story. You may look at the passages, or sources, when you think it would be helpful. You may also look at your notes.

GO ON →

Source #1: Service Dogs

What do service dogs do?

Service dogs help people live good lives. They can open doors for people who need help. They can warn people who cannot hear sirens. They can help people walk. Service dogs and their owners are a team. Their owners love them, and they love their owners.

How do dogs learn how to help people?

Service dogs need teachers just like people do. Trainers teach the dogs to stay calm. They teach the dogs how to look and listen for danger. They teach the dogs how to help their owners.

When do service dogs start working?

Service dogs are trained for six months. Their new owners also must learn how to work with them. Then the dogs start helping their owners.

Dogs are true, loving friends. They work hard. They are smart. Dogs can keep people from being hurt. They can help people get around safely. They become part of their owners' families. Their owners can do more things because of them.

GO ON →

Source #2: Helping Each Other

There are lots of animals that help people. Service animals help people stay safe and get around. Police dogs can help find lost people. They can also sniff out danger. Before there were cars, horses used to help people get around. House pets help keep people from feeling lonely.

What do people do for animals? Some people, like Eve Fertig, do a lot. When Eve was young, her father took in stray animals. He took care of hurt animals and found homes for them. Eve helped him. When she grew up, she remembered the animals her father had helped. She decided to help animals, too.

Now Eve takes care of any animals that need help. She even takes care of wild animals. Eve has another job, too. She teaches people how to take care of hurt animals. Eve hopes that some of these people will continue her work.

Has Eve ever been helped by an animal? Yes, she has. She and her husband adopted a dog named Shana. One evening, they were outside and got caught in a storm. Trees fell. They were trapped. Shana dug a tunnel and rescued them. When they got home, they had no power. Shana kept them warm all night.

GO ON →

Student Name _____

1   Pick **two** choices that show details found in **both** "Service Dogs" and "Helping Each Other."

    A Dogs can dig tunnels.

    B Dogs can keep people safe.

    C Dogs can find lost people.

    D Dogs can live in the wild.

    E Dogs can be part of a family.

2   Tell **two** different ways that animals help people. Give **one** example from **each** source. Be sure to give the title of the article for each example.

_____

_____

_____

_____

_____

_____

GO ON →

Student Name _____

3 "Service Dogs" and "Helping Each Other" tell how people and animals help each other. Why is this idea important? Use **one** example from **each** source in your answer. Be sure to give the title of the article for each example.

_____

_____

_____

_____

_____

GO ON →

Directions for Part 2

You will now look at your sources. You will take notes. Then you will plan, draft, revise, and edit your story for the class book. First read your assignment and the information about how your story will be scored. Then begin your work.

Your Assignment:

Your class is creating a class book about people and animals helping each other. Your assignment is to write a story for the book about how you might help an animal or how an animal might help you. Your story will be read by other students, teachers, parents, and other people who read the class book.

Using information from the two sources, "Service Dogs" and "Helping Each Other," write a story about how you might help an animal or how an animal might help you. It must be several paragraphs long. The story will let students in your class know how people and animals can help each other. Include information from both sources using your own words. Be sure to write who the story is about, where your story takes place, and what happens.

REMEMBER: A well-written story

- is well-organized and stays on the topic
- has an introduction and conclusion
- uses details from the sources
- develops ideas fully
- uses clear language
- follows rules of writing (spelling, punctuation, and grammar)

Now begin work on your story. Manage your time carefully so that you can plan, write, revise, and edit your story. Write your response on a separate sheet of paper.

STOP

Read the passage. Then answer the questions.

Up with Kites!

It is fun to fly a kite on a windy day. But kites are not just toys. People have used kites in many ways.

The first kites were made over 2,000 years ago. They were made in China. They were used to send messages. A kite's color and movements were like words. Soldiers at war used kites to talk to friends who were far away. Children in China began to fly kites, too. Very old pictures show children flying kites.

From China, kites came to other parts of the world. About 700 years ago, a man went to China from Europe for the first time. His name was Marco Polo. He brought many things back to Europe. He also brought stories about Chinese kites.

The rider uses a kite to pull the beach buggy.

GO ON →

You may be surprised at the ways kites have helped people. You know some people flew kites to talk. Others used kites to catch fish. They attached fishing line to a kite. Then they flew the kite over water. Sending a kite over water helped people build bridges, too. Building bridges was hard. Getting the first line across was the hardest part. With a kite, the job was much easier. Kites were also used to pull wagons and boats. In 1999, kites even pulled sleds to the North Pole!

Scientists have used kites to learn about weather. Do you know about Ben Franklin and his kite? Long ago, Ben Franklin wanted to know if lightning was electricity. He learned by flying a kite. He flew his kite in a storm. Flying a kite in a storm is not safe. But Franklin was lucky. He did not get hurt. The U.S. Weather Service has also used kites. They put tools to tell about the weather in kites. They used kites to send cameras up into the sky, too.

Some kites are big and strong. During World War I, people were lifted in large box kites. A soldier high in the sky could see very far. The soldier could see what was happening far away. Kites were used again during World War II. Sometimes soldiers got lost at sea. So they sent up kites to call for help. Kites saved many people!

Around 1900, people wanted to build a flying machine. They studied kites. Alexander Graham Bell made large kites. These kites could carry a person. The Wright brothers made and flew kites, too. They watched the way birds fly. They learned about the wind. They tried to ride on kites. Then in 1903, the Wright brothers made the first airplane. Without kites, there would be no airplanes!

GO ON →

1 Which sentence **best** states the main idea of the passage?

   A It is fun to fly a kite on a windy day.

   B People have used kites in many ways.

   C The first kites were made over 2,000 years ago.

   D A kite's color and movements were like words.

2 Read the sentence from the passage.

They attached fishing <u>line</u> to a kite.

Which is the **best** meaning of the word <u>line</u> in this sentence?

   A something you draw on paper

   B the edge of something

   C people standing behind each other

   D a strong, thin string or rope

3 Draw a line to match **each** word from the passage on the left with the word on the right that means the opposite.

first		went
far		push
came		last
pull		near

GO ON →

4   What **two** ways have kites helped people? Use details
from the passage in your answer.

_____

_____

_____

_____

_____

5   Read the sentences from the passage.

Flying a kite in a storm is not safe. But Franklin was <u>lucky</u>.

What does the word <u>lucky</u> tell about Benjamin Franklin?

   A He did not care about luck.

   B He did not have good luck.

   C He had good luck.

   D He needed good luck.

GO ON →

6 The following question has two parts. First, answer part A. Then, answer part B.

Part A: Read the paragraph from the passage.

Around 1900, people wanted to build a flying machine. They studied kites. Alexander Graham Bell made large kites. These kites could carry a person. The Wright brothers made and flew kites, too. They watched the way birds fly. They learned about the wind. They tried to ride on kites. Then in 1903, the Wright brothers made the first airplane. Without kites, there would be no airplanes!

What is the main idea of this paragraph?

A Long ago, people built huge kites.

B Alexander Graham Bell was interested in kites.

C Kites were used by those who invented the airplane.

D The Wright brothers studied how birds flew through the air.

Part B: Which sentence from the paragraph **best** helps you answer part A?

A Around 1900, people wanted to build a flying machine.

B These kites could carry a person.

C They learned about the wind.

D Without kites, there would be no airplanes!

GO ON →

Read the passage. Then answer the questions.

The Wolf and the Crane

A long time ago, a wolf was eating when a bone got stuck in his throat. He could not get the bone down. He could not get the bone up. Worst of all, he could not finish eating!

The wolf had to get help. He hurried off to see the crane. The crane was a bird with a long, thin neck. She also had a long, thin beak. He knew she could reach the bone and pull it out.

The wolf found the crane at the river. She was looking for fish to eat. The crane was as still as a rock. She was staring down at the water around her feet.

"Crane!" the wolf growled. She jumped up into the air, flapping her wings in surprise. "I need your help," he said. "You must pull this bone out of my throat. Quickly!"

The crane was not sure what to do. She usually flew away when she saw the wolf. She was also very scared to put her head in the wolf's throat.

"Why should I help you?" the crane asked.

The wolf thought for a minute. "Well," he said. "I will reward you for it. That is why!"

GO ON →

The crane flapped her wings again, but this time in excitement. A reward! What could it be? The crane thought of a large pile of fish. It would be very tasty. Then she thought of his fluffy fur. It would make her nest very soft.

The crane moved closer to the wolf. "I will do it," she said.

And so, the wolf leaned back. He opened his mouth as wide as he could. The crane leaned down. She put her beak, head, and neck into his throat. A few moments later, she pulled out her neck. Then she pulled out her head and beak. In her beak was the bone that had been stuck!

The crane danced around proudly. She had done what the wolf had asked. Now she would get fish, or fur, or another reward.

She looked at the wolf. But the wolf simply turned to walk away.

"Wait!" the crane called after him. "You said you would give me a reward."

"What?!" the wolf hissed as he swung around, causing the crane to jump up into a tree. "Haven't you gotten your reward? Isn't it enough that I let you take your head out of my mouth without snapping it off?"

The crane watched from the tree as the wolf walked away. She saw she had made a mistake in trusting such a bad, mean animal. As she flew away, she told herself never to do that again.

GO ON →

7 The following question has two parts. First, answer part A. Then, answer part B.

Part A: What problem does the wolf have to solve?

A He cannot find food.

B He cannot find the crane.

C He cannot get a reward for the crane.

D He cannot get a bone out of his throat.

Part B: Which sentence from the passage **best** tells how the crane solves the wolf's problem?

A She usually flew away when she saw the wolf.

B The crane moved closer to the wolf.

C In her beak was the bone that had been stuck!

D Now she would get fish, or fur, or another reward.

8 Read the sentence from the passage.

The crane thought of a <u>large</u> pile of fish.

Which **two** words below mean the opposite of <u>large</u>?

A old

B cold

C small

D hard

E tiny

GO ON →

9 What happens in the beginning, middle, and end of the passage? Mark an X in **one** box for **each** part of the passage.

	Beginning	Middle	End
The crane learns a lesson.	☐	☐	☐
The wolf goes to see the crane.	☐	☐	☐
The crane helps the wolf.	☐	☐	☐

10 Read the sentence from the passage.

The crane danced around <u>proudly</u>.

What does the word <u>proudly</u> **most likely** mean?

A not proud

B in a proud way

C proud again

D one who is proud

GO ON →

Read the poem. Then answer the questions.

Steel Gray Bird

Steel
Gray bird
In the night,
With your beam
Do   That shines so bright,
you have a place to be? Someplace special you will see?
I watch you, and I wonder why you move so slowly in the sky.
Tired but with work to do, you're always off to somewhere new.
But maybe someday
Very soon I'll fly
With you to
Touch the
Moon!

GO ON →

11 What is the speaker doing in the poem?

    A flying with a bird

    B looking up at the sky

    C shining a light

    D dreaming in bed

12 Read the lines from the poem. Draw a circle around the **two** words that rhyme.

Steel

Gray bird

In the night,

With your beam

That shines so bright,

GO ON →

13   Read the line from the poem.

I <u>watch</u> you, and I wonder why you move so slowly in the sky.

What is the meaning of the word <u>watch</u> in the line?

A   look at

B   clock

C   wait for

D   time

14   Where does the speaker want to go?

A   to school

B   to the clouds

C   to the Moon

D   to Mars

15   What does the reader learn from the shape of the poem?

A   what the speaker sees

B   which words in the poem rhyme

C   when the poem was written

D   who the speaker is

GO ON →

The draft below needs revision. Read the draft. Then answer the questions.

The Pond

(1) The town pond is a special place. (2) It is fun to visit all year long. (3) There is always something to do.

(4) In summer, you can go to see the swans. (5) People sit on the benchs. (6) The swans look very funny when they walk around among the people.

(7) In fall, the leaves turn colors. (8) It so pretty! (9) People like to look at the trees.

(10) In winter, the pond freezes. (11) The pond gets busy on sundays because everyone wants to go skating.

(12) Spring is one of the best times of the year to go to the pond. (13) It is when all the baby animals are born. (14) You can find baby birds turtles and chipmunks. (15) One year, I even found baby mouses! (16) The grass is green and flowers grow. (17) I love the pond the most in spring!

GO ON →

16 What is the **best** way to write sentence 5?

 A People sit on the benchs.

 B People sit on the benches.

 C People sit on the Benches.

 D people sit on the benches.

17 What is the **best** way to write sentence 8?

 A Its so pretty!

 B I'ts so pretty!

 C Its' so pretty!

 D It's so pretty!

18 What is the correct way to write sentence 11?

 A The pond gets busy on Sundays because everyone wants to go skating.

 B The pond gets busy on Sundays because Everyone wants to go skating.

 C The ponds gets busy on Sundays because everyone wants to go skating.

 D The pond gets busy on sundays because everyone wants to go skating.

GO ON →

19 What is the correct way to write sentence 14?

    A You can find, baby birds turtles and chipmunks.

    B You can find baby birds turtles, and chipmunks.

    C You can find baby birds turtles and, chipmunks.

    D You can find baby birds, turtles, and chipmunks.

20 What is the **best** way to write sentence 15?

    A One Year, I even found baby mouses!

    B One year, I even found babies mice!

    C One year, I even found baby mice!

    D One year, I even found baby mouses!

GO ON →

Answer these questions.

21 Which word has the same long <u>o</u> vowel sound as <u>rope</u>?

    A rock

    B hop

    C drove

22 Which word has the same long <u>u</u> vowel sound as <u>cube</u>?

    A mule

    B cut

    C rut

23 Which word has the same end sound as <u>ledge</u>?

    A led

    B cage

    C gem

GO ON →

Student Name _____

24 Which word has the same end sound as <u>witch</u>?

    A wit

    B watch

    C wash

25 Which word has the same three-letter blend as <u>strong</u>?

    A spring

    B wrong

    C strict

Informational Performance Task

Task:

Your class has been learning about how animals play a part in the world around us. Your teacher has asked you to write an informational article for a class book on animals.

Before you decide what you will write about, you will read two passages, or sources, that provide information about zebras and giraffes. After you have looked at these passages, or sources, you will answer some questions about them. Look at the passages and the three questions that follow. Then, go back and read the passages carefully. They will give you the information you will need to answer the questions and write an informational article.

In Part 2, you will write an informational article using information from the two passages.

Directions for Part 1

You will now look at two passages, or sources. You can look at either of the passages as often as you like.

Research Questions:

After looking at the passages, use the rest of the time in Part 1 to answer three questions about them. Your answers to these questions will be scored. Also, your answers will help you think about the information you have read, which should help you write your informational article. You may look at the passages, or sources, when you think they would be helpful. You may also look at your notes.

GO ON →

Source #1: A Horse of a Different Color

Did you know that in the past zebras were called horse tigers? People thought a zebra was a mix of a horse and a tiger. Zebras are interesting animals!

Stripes

Zebras look a lot like horses. They have white coats with black stripes. Every zebra has different stripes. We don't know for sure why they have stripes. The stripes might help keep them safe.

Families

Zebras live in Africa. They live in family groups. Each family has one grownup male and a few grownup females. There are many young zebras in a family. Families join together to make a herd. A herd has hundreds of members.

Babies

Baby zebras are called foals. They have white bodies with brown stripes. Their stripes turn black as they get older. Their fur is soft and fuzzy. Babies can walk 20 minutes after birth. They run when they are an hour old. Mothers keep their babies away from other zebras until the babies are a few days old. Each baby knows its mother by her stripes.

Dangers

Life can be dangerous for zebras. Lions and wild dogs are their enemies. Zebras have ways to stay safe. Their stripes help them. The stripes make them look blurry when they run. They can run fast. Their enemies may not see them. They fight their enemies by kicking. Zebra family members protect each other.

GO ON →

Source #2: Giraffes

People once thought a giraffe was part camel and part leopard. Giraffes were called camel leopards. Their real name is *camelopardalis*. This means "fast walking camel leopard."

Tall Animals

Why do animals look up to giraffes? They are the tallest animals in the world. They could look into a second-floor window! A giraffe's legs are taller than most people. Giraffes have white or tan coats with spots. Each giraffe's coat looks different.

Herds

Giraffes live in Africa. Most live in small groups called herds. Some herds have grownup females and young giraffes. Other herds have grownup males. Some grownup males live alone.

Babies

Baby giraffes are called calves. The calves are taller when born than most grownup people. In less than an hour after birth, the calves can walk. They can run when only 10 hours old. Calves are never left alone. They are watched over by grownup females.

Staying Safe

Lions and crocodiles are giraffes' enemies. Giraffes' bodies help keep them safe. They have spotted coats. Their coats help them blend in with trees. Their enemies may not see them. Being tall also helps. They can see enemies that are far away. They can run fast. Their enemies can't catch them. Giraffes protect themselves. They fight their enemies with strong kicks.

GO ON →

Student Name _____

1   Pick **two** choices that show ideas about animals found in **both** "A Horse of a Different Color" and "Giraffes."

     A   Animal coats help animals hide from their enemies.

     B   Animals make noises to scare away other animals.

     C   Animal babies can walk soon after they are born.

     D   Animal babies live with their mother and father.

     E   Animals all look the same.

2   "A Horse of a Different Color" and "Giraffes" give information about zebras and giraffes. Write a paragraph that tells in your own words at least **two** facts you have learned about baby zebras and baby giraffes. Use at least **one** detail from **each** source in your answer. Be sure to give the title of the source for each detail.

_____

_____

_____

_____

_____

GO ON →

3   How do zebras' and giraffes' bodies help keep these animals safe? In your answer, use at least **one** detail from **each** source, "A Horse of a Different Color" and "Giraffes." Be sure to give the title of the source for each detail.

_____

_____

_____

_____

_____

GO ON →

Directions for Part 2

You will now look at your passages, or sources. You will take notes. Then you will plan, draft, revise, and edit your article. First read your assignment and the information about how your informational article will be scored. Then begin your work.

Your Assignment:

Your class has been learning about how animals play a part in the world around us. Your assignment is to write an informational article that uses information about what you have learned about zebras and giraffes.

Using information from the two sources, "A Horse of a Different Color" and "Giraffes," write an informational article telling how zebras and giraffes are alike and how they are different.

Your article must be several paragraphs long. Make sure to have a main idea. Support your main idea with details from both sources. Remember to use your own words. Be sure to state your ideas clearly.

REMEMBER: A well-written informational article

- has a clear main idea
- is well-organized and stays on the topic
- has an introduction and conclusion
- uses transitions
- uses details from the sources to support your main idea
- develops ideas fully
- uses clear language
- follows rules of writing (spelling, punctuation, and grammar)

Now begin work on your informational article. Manage your time carefully so that you can plan, write, revise, and edit your article. Write your response on a separate sheet of paper.

STOP

Read the passage. Then answer the questions.

Rocketi the Cheetah

It can be hard to have lots of brothers and sisters. Just ask Rocketi. She is a cheetah that was born at a wildlife center in Texas.

Rocketi's mother did not have enough milk to feed all six of her babies. Rocketi was pushed away by her brothers and sisters. She did not get enough to eat.

The workers at the wildlife center wanted to help Rocketi. They wanted to give her a chance to survive. So, Rocketi moved to an animal park in California.

Rocketi was a hungry cub. The zookeepers fed her a giant bottle of special milk four times a day. She began to grow and gain weight.

She also began to think of her human keepers as her family. She would run around the nursery and play with them. One of her favorite games was tug of war.

In 2018, Rocketi was big enough to move to the San Diego Zoo. This zoo is known for its animal ambassadors. These are animals that walk around the zoo and let visitors look at them. They help teach people to value animals.

Wild cheetahs distrust humans. But Rocketi thinks of humans as her friends. Meeting people while she walks around the zoo will not bother her at all. Rocketi will make a wonderful animal ambassador!

GO ON →

1 The following question has two parts. First, answer part A. Then, answer part B.

Part A: Which sentence **best** states the main idea of the passage?

A Rocketi's brothers and sisters pushed her away.

B Animal ambassadors teach people to value animals.

C Rocketi moved from Texas to California.

D People worked together to raise a cheetah cub.

Part B: Which sentence from the passage **best** helps you answer part A?

A It can be hard to have lots of brothers and sisters.

B The workers at the wildlife center wanted to help Rocketi.

C The zoo is known for its animal ambassadors.

D But Rocketi thinks of humans as her friends.

2 Read the sentence from the passage.

Wild cheetahs <u>distrust</u> humans.

What does the word <u>distrust</u> mean?

A the opposite of trust

B wrongly trust

C someone who trusts

D trust again

GO ON →

3   Read the sentences from the passage.

The workers at the wildlife center wanted to help Rocketi. They wanted to give her a chance to <u>survive</u>.

Draw **two** lines to match the word <u>survive</u> to **two** words that have almost the same meaning.

continue

grow

survive   eat

live

play

4   Why did the author **mostly likely** write this passage?

   A   to describe the life of a cheetah cub

   B   to get readers to visit the San Diego Zoo

   C   to give steps for how to raise a cheetah

   D   to teach readers about animal ambassadors

GO ON →

Read the passage. Then answer the questions.

A New Friend

I watched the moving men unload the truck. Mom and Dad were busy inside the new house. So was my sister. She was excited about fixing up her new bedroom, but I thought the yard and the neighborhood were more interesting. I like to run, jump, and play ball. Most of all, I like to ride Harriet, my trusty blue bike. Coasting along on Harriet, I feel as free as the wind—and as strong!

But right then I was not feeling strong. I thought about my old neighborhood. Our new town felt strange, and I barely knew my way around the block. All morning there was a lump in my throat. A few times I had to blink back tears. But I had not cried since I was four, and I was not going to start.

Everything would be fine as soon as I could ride Harriet. But Harriet, along with everything else we owned, had disappeared into the big truck early this morning. I went to the driveway every few minutes to recheck if they had brought her out.

GO ON →

At last, one of the men poked his head out of the back of the truck. "Anybody out here need a bike?" he teased. "I have a pretty blue bike for sale. It comes with a nice big basket, too."

He handed Harriet down, and in two seconds we were off. I pumped the pedals to get some speed. We circled the block, and then I slowed down and looked around. I wanted to learn about my new neighborhood.

On my second time around the block, I saw an amazing garden. Then I saw an old man. He was on his knees doing something with a plant. It looked like he was digging it up. The plant was covered with red flowers. Why would anyone dig up such a beautiful plant? I squeezed the brakes and stopped to find out.

"Hello, I am Noor. I am new here," I said. "I love your garden!"

The man looked up and grinned. "Hello, Noor," he said. "I am Mr. Paz. I am happy to see a new family move in. This plant is for your yard. I have dug it up, but I do not know how I will be able to carry it." He pointed to another plant. "I dug up that one, too. You can see the roots. That is for Mrs. Alba in the house next to yours. It is a surprise for her birthday." He looked a little sad. "I do not know how I will be able to move that one, either."

"Harriet can do it! The plants will fit right here," I said, pointing to Harriet's basket.

"Who is Harriet, and does she ride your lovely bike?" asked Mr. Paz.

I laughed and rubbed the handlebars. "This is Harriet. I will ride her, and she will carry the plants. If you need something at the store, we can carry that, too."

So that is how I made my first new friend. And that is how I got started doing errands for Mr. Paz.

GO ON →

5   Read the sentence from the passage.

I went to the driveway every few minutes to <u>recheck</u> if they had brought her out.

What is the meaning of the word <u>recheck</u> in the sentence?

A   not check

B   check before

C   check again

D   able to check

6   What is the number order of the events in the passage? Mark an X in **one** box for **each** event.

	1	2	3	4
Noor waits for Harriet to get off the truck.	☐	☐	☐	☐
Noor offers to carry plants in Harriet's basket.	☐	☐	☐	☐
Noor sees Mr. Paz in his garden.	☐	☐	☐	☐
Noor begins to ride around the block on Harriet.	☐	☐	☐	☐

GO ON →

7   Read the sentence from the passage.

The man looked up and <u>grinned.</u>

What is another word for <u>grinned</u>?

A lifted

B smiled

C stood

D went

8   What happens before Noor starts to ride her bicycle? Use **two** details from the passage in your answer.

_____

_____

_____

_____

_____

9   Which sentence from the passage has a compound word?

A I watched the moving men unload the truck.

B I pumped the pedals to get some speed.

C I squeezed the brakes and stopped to find out.

D I laughed and rubbed the handlebars.   **GO ON →**

Read the passage. Then answer the questions.

The Saguaro Cactus

The saguaro cactus is a wonderful plant. It lives in a difficult place, but it has ways to stay alive. It is known for its beautiful flowers and for being very tall. The saguaro is the largest cactus in the United States!

Staying Alive in the Desert

Saguaros are found in the desert, which is a hot, dry place. There is not much water in the desert. Plants and animals need water to live, so not many plants live in the desert. A cactus is one plant that can live there. Cactus plants store water inside their stems. This helps them live through long periods with no rain.

Sometimes very strong winds blow through the desert. Saguaros stay standing because they have strong roots, which keep them firmly in the ground. The roots are important. The roots can get cut when people dig into the ground to make roads. This can kill the saguaro

How a Saguaro Grows

A saguaro can grow as tall as 50 feet high. However, it takes a long time for a saguaro to grow. A healthy saguaro can live for more than 100 years.

GO ON →

The Growth of the Saguaro

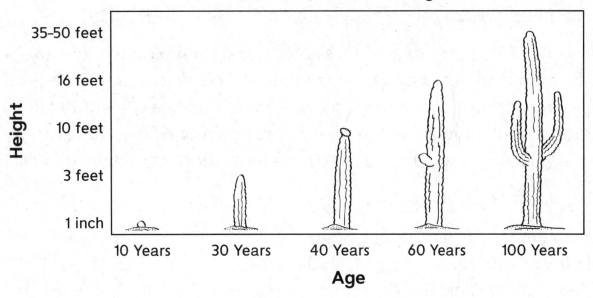

The saguaro blooms in spring. Its flowers are beautiful. But the saguaro is more than just a pretty plant. Animals use the saguaro for shade from the hot desert sun. Many animals eat the fruit of the saguaro. They drink the juice and eat the seeds. This helps the animals stay alive and helps the saguaro. Animals spread the seeds to other parts of the desert. This is how new saguaro plants are planted and begin to grow.

Saguaro National Park

President Herbert Hoover set aside land in Arizona for the saguaro cactus. That land became Saguaro National Park in the Sonoran Desert. It is a place to keep saguaros safe. There are more than a million saguaros in the park. Park workers study the plants to learn more about how they grow.

GO ON →

Volunteers in the park collect money to protect saguaros. The Adopt-a-Saguaro program raises money to save these plants.

People give money to adopt a saguaro, and then park workers use the money to take care of the saguaro. People who adopt them get pictures of their saguaros. A second-grade class was one of the first groups that adopted a saguaro. They raised money by selling things at a yard sale. More than 100 schools have adopted saguaros.

Saguaros with Microchips

Some money from Adopt-a-Saguaro helps to stop thieves who steal saguaros. The park workers use the money to buy microchips. They put the microchips into saguaros. Microchips are tiny computer parts that store information. The chip is about the size of a grain of rice. It stores facts about a cactus and tells where the cactus is in the park. If someone finds a

Park workers place microchips like this one into saguaros.

saguaro with a microchip that is not in the park, they know it is stolen. The chip also stores information about the size and health of the saguaro.

Groups work hard to protect the saguaro and to teach others about this special plant. If people work together, saguaros can stay healthy and grow tall and strong.

GO ON →

10 Draw a line between **each** question and its matching answer. Not all answers will be used.

The animals eat the saguaro fruit.

How do animals help the saguaro?

The animals see the saguaro flowers.

The animals spread saguaro seeds.

How does the saguaro help animals?

The animals keep saguaro safe.

11 Under which heading in the passage can readers find information about why saguaro roots are important?

A Staying Alive in the Desert

B How a Saguaro Grows

C Saguaro National Park

D Saguaros with Microchips

12 Which word from the passage is a compound word?

A workers

B protect

C adopted

D someone

GO ON →

13 What can readers learn from the bar graph?

    A how long the oldest saguaro lived

    B the tallest saguaro that is alive today

    C how tall a saguaro is at different ages

    D the greatest height of a saguaro

14 What does the diagram of a microchip show?

    A how much smaller a microchip is than a saguaro

    B that a microchip can store a lot of facts

    C where a microchip can be bought

    D what a microchip looks like

15 What are the **most likely** reasons that the author wrote this passage? Pick **two** choices.

    A to share facts about saguaros

    B to get readers to adopt a saguaro

    C to tell why President Hoover liked saguaros

    D to prove the saguaro is the best cactus of all

    E to give facts about how people help to protect saguaros

GO ON →

The draft below needs revision. Read the draft. Then answer the questions.

The Corn Palace

(1) Last summer, my family drove to South Dakota. (2) On the way, we stopped to see the Corn Palace. (3) What is the Corn Palace. (4) The Corn Palace is a place that is decorated with murals, or pictures. (5) The murals are made from corn.

(6) When I think of corn, I think of the color yellow. (7) I found out right away that there are a whole rainbow of corn colors. (8) One mural had red green, and blue corn. (9) There were other colors, too.

(10) Dad says the murals always has a theme. (11) The theme is different every year. (12) The theme we saw was "South Dakota Weather." (13) We saw pictures of a snowman and colorful fall trees. (14) My favorite mural was the tornado!

(15) When we will leave, Dad told us something funny. (16) Some people call the Corn Palace the world's largest bird feeder. (17) Hungry birds peck on the corn murals for food in the winter. (18) At least someone gets to eat all that corn!

GO ON →

16   What is the correct way to write sentence 3?

    A   what is the Corn Palace?

    B   What are the Corn Palace.

    C   What is the Corn Palace?

    D   What is the Corn Palace.

17   What is the **best** way to write sentence 7?

    A   I found out right away that there is a whole rainbow of corn colors.

    B   I found out right away that there are a whole Rainbow of corn colors.

    C   I found out right away that there is a whole rainbow of Corn colors.

    D   I found out right away that there are a whole rainbow of corn colors.

18   What is the correct way to write sentence 8?

    A   One mural had red green and blue trim.

    B   One mural had red, green, and, blue trim.

    C   One mural had, red, green and blue trim.

    D   One mural had red, green, and blue trim.

GO ON →

19 What is the **best** way to write sentence 10?

    A dad says the murals always have a theme.

    B Dad says the murals always has a theme.

    C Dad says the murals always have a theme.

    D Dad says the murals always has a theme?

20 What is the correct way to write sentence 15?

    A When they will leave, Dad told us something funny.

    B When we left, Dad told us something funny.

    C When we will leave, dad told us something funny.

    D When we left, Dad told us something funny?

GO ON →

Answer these questions.

21 Which word has the same vowel sound as <u>rain</u>?

    A ran

    B weigh

    C graph

22 Which word has the same vowel sound as <u>my</u>?

    A me

    B may

    C might

23 Which word has the same vowel sound as <u>so</u>?

    A slow

    B stop

    C son

GO ON →

Student Name _____

24 Which word has the same vowel sound as <u>key</u>?

    A ten

    B tree

    C tie

25 Which word has the same vowel sound as <u>few</u>?

    A she

    B fun

    C mute

Opinion Performance Task

Task:

Your class has been learning about living in a world full of surprises. Your teacher has asked you to write an opinion article about which is more important, mail service or telephones.

Before you decide what you will write about, you will read two passages, or sources, that provide information about the history of the mail service and the telephone service. After you have read these passages, or sources, you will answer some questions about them. Look at the passages and the three questions that follow. Then, go back and read the passages carefully. They will give you the information you will need to answer the questions and write an opinion article.

In Part 2, you will write an opinion article using information from the two passages.

Directions for Part 1

You will now look at two passages, or sources. You can look at either of the passages as often as you like.

Research Questions:

After looking at the passages, use the rest of the time in Part 1 to answer three questions about them. Your answers to these questions will be scored. Also, your answers will help you think about the information you have read, which should help you write your opinion article. You may look at the passages, or sources, when you think they would be helpful. You may also look at your notes.

GO ON →

Source #1: The Mail Is Here!

The United States Postal Service has been bringing mail to the people of our country for over 200 years. Today cars and trucks carry mail. Trains, planes, and ships bring letters to faraway places. Some mail can reach people in less than a day. People from long ago never dreamed the mail would move that fast!

Getting and sending letters used to be very hard. There were few roads between villages or towns. There was not a group of people to carry the mail. People talked to their neighbors. They found out who was making a trip out of the village. Those travelers carried the mail with them on their trip. Letters took weeks or months to be delivered. Some letters never arrived. It was hard to share news with others.

Soon more people from other countries came to live in America. Cities and towns grew. Roads were built. These roads made it easier to go from one place to another. Post offices were built. People went there to send or pick up mail. Men called post riders carried the mail. They rode on horseback or drove wagons. They rode through storms. They rode through snow. They had an important job. People were waiting for the mail to come.

A group of horseback riders carried mail to the people in the west. They were called the Pony Express. These riders made the horses run very fast. When the horses got tired, the riders stopped and got different horses. This helped them carry the mail quickly.

GO ON →

Mail service changed when cars were made. Mail could be brought right to people's homes. Mail carriers drove to neighborhoods and farms. They brought mail to people who lived far away from a city. The mail carrier could even pick up letters that needed to be sent. Sending and receiving mail became easy.

The mail service in America has changed over the years. Through all of the changes, one thing has stayed the same. Mail helps us to share news with friends and family all over the world.

GO ON →

Source #2: Bell's Telephone

"Mr. Watson, come here. I want to see you." These words were said on March 10, 1876, by Alexander Graham Bell. He was testing the telephone that he had built. His helper, Thomas Watson, was in a different room. Watson was able to hear the words that were carried through an electrical wire. Their work changed the world!

Alexander Graham Bell was born in Scotland in 1847. Alexander's father was a teacher. He taught Alexander how a person's voice works. He taught him about sound. Alexander wanted to know about sound because his mother was deaf. People who are deaf cannot hear. Alexander wanted deaf people to be able to share messages with others.

The Bell family moved to Canada when Alexander was a young man. Alexander was still learning about sound. He studied and built things that he hoped would help others. Then he moved to America and taught in a school for the deaf. When he was not teaching, he worked on his projects. Bell thought that he could find a way to make spoken words travel across an electrical wire.

Some men found out that Bell was trying to build a telephone. They wanted to help. They gave him money so that he could get a helper. Bell hired his friend, Thomas Watson. The two men worked for many hours testing the telephone. Alexander did not want to give up on his dream. Finally, the machine worked! The men took turns speaking to each other over the telephone.

GO ON →

The news about the telephone was told all around the world. People were excited about the new invention. They wanted to know how it worked. They wanted to buy a telephone so that they could talk to people. In just ten years, more than 150,000 people in America had a telephone.

Bell believed that the telephone would change over time. He was right. People have worked to make telephones better. Telephone calls used to be made only from inside a building. Telephones used electricity that came through wires in a building. Today, cell phones are powered by batteries. They can be used almost anywhere. People can even see each other on their phones while they talk! The telephone keeps getting better and better.

GO ON →

1   Which ideas tell what **both** "The Mail Is Here!" and "Bell's Telephone" say about people's lives? Pick **two** choices.

   A   People should write more letters and talk less.

   B   People can make changes that will help others.

   C   People spend too much time trying new things.

   D   People want to be able to stay in contact with others.

   E   People think the mail service is not as important as cell phones.

2   Explain what **both** sources say about how people felt about keeping in touch with family and friends. Use **one** detail from **each** source to support your explanation. Be sure to give the title of the source for each detail.

   _____

   _____

   _____

   _____

   _____

   _____

GO ON →

3   Explain what the world would be like if no one had
worked to make it easier to share news with others. Use
one detail from "The Mail Is Here!" and **one** detail from
"Bell's Telephone" in your answer. For each detail, include
the source name or number.

_____

_____

_____

_____

_____

_____

GO ON →

Directions for Part 2

You will now look at your passages, or sources. You will take notes. Then, you will plan, draft, revise, and edit your opinion article. First read your assignment and the information about how your opinion article will be scored. Then begin your work.

Your Assignment:

Your teacher wants everyone in class to write an opinion article about which is the most important, mail service or telephones. Use information from the two passages, "The Mail Is Here!" and "Bell's Telephone," to support your opinion article. In your article, state and support your opinion about which service you think is more important.

Your article must be several paragraphs long. Make sure to give a clear opinion. Support your opinion with details from the sources. Remember to use your own words. Be sure to state your ideas clearly.

REMEMBER: A well-written opinion article

- has a clear opinion
- is well-organized and stays on the topic
- has an introduction and conclusion
- uses transitions
- uses details from the sources to support your opinion
- develops ideas fully
- uses clear language
- follows rules of writing (spelling, punctuation, and grammar)

Now begin work on your opinion article. Manage your time carefully so that you can plan, write, revise, and edit your article. Write your response on a separate sheet of paper.

Read the passage. Then answer the questions.

Cleaning Up the Park

The sun was shining, and the trees were full of green leaves and singing birds. It was a beautiful day to be at the park.

"Today I can taste springtime," said Liam. We both leaned forward on the bench we were sitting on, enjoying the sight of the flowers at our feet. They were a promise of even warmer days to come.

"One thing I know I can taste is this ice cream," I said, as I popped the last bite in my mouth and walked toward the trash can. Liam shoved the rest of his cone in his mouth. Then he ran toward the slide. As he ran, his napkin dropped to the ground. "You dropped your napkin," I called.

"Who cares?" Liam called while he happily climbed the slide.

"I care," I said quietly. I picked up Liam's napkin and angrily threw it in the trash. I was not sure why I felt angry, but then I looked back up at the trees and listened to the birds and thought about how even one napkin can hurt Earth.

"Why are you upset?" asked Liam when he saw the frown on my face. "It was just one napkin."

I took a big breath and started talking: "Liam, if each person dropped a napkin on the ground, the park would be covered in napkins. There are at least twenty kids here. Think about what the park would look like with twenty napkins on the ground."

GO ON →

"That would be pretty messy," Liam said.

"It's not just messy," I said. "It's bad for our planet. Some of the trash you drop at the playground can hurt plants and animals. I know you care about Earth, but you have to take care of Earth, too."

Liam suddenly ran off. I was not sure where he was going, but then I saw him grab a piece of trash. I joined Liam, and together we picked up napkins and snack wrappers.

"I guess other kids don't know how bad one piece of trash can be," said Liam. "I wish we could teach them how easy it is to take care of Earth."

I thought for a moment and then had an idea. "Do you want to plan a park clean-up day with me?" I asked.

Liam's face lit up. "We can invite our friends. Together we can make our park a better place. And our planet, too!"

GO ON →

Student Name _____

1   At the beginning of the passage, Liam and the speaker think differently about throwing trash on the ground. What does Liam think about throwing trash on the ground? What does the speaker think? Use details from the passage in your answer.

_____

_____

_____

_____

_____

2   Read the sentence from the passage.

We both <u>leaned</u> forward on the bench we were sitting on, enjoying the sight of the flowers at our feet.

Which word from the sentence best helps you understand what <u>leaned</u> means?

A forward

B bench

C sight

D feet

GO ON →

3 This question has two parts. First, answer part A. Then, answer part B.

Part A: At the end of the story, what do **both** Liam and the speaker want to do?"

A Tell the kids at the park to clean up their mess.

B Go find another park to play in and clean up.

C Plan a day for people to help clean up the park.

D Get a reward for cleaning up the park.

Part B: Which sentence from the passage **best** helps you answer part A?

A "Some of the trash you drop at the playground can hurt plants and animals."

B I was not sure where he was going, but then I saw him grab a piece of trash.

C I thought for a moment and then had an idea.

D "Together we can make our park a better place."

GO ON →

4 Read the sentence from the passage.

"That would be pretty <u>messy</u>," Liam said.

Which **two** words mean the opposite of <u>messy</u>?

A neat

B useful

C easy

D dirty

E orderly

5 Which statement **best** describes a main theme of the passage?

A True friends help each other with everything.

B Each person's actions either hurt the planet or help it.

C When you help others, you help yourself, too.

D If everyone leaves a napkin, there will not be enough napkins.

GO ON →

6 This question has two parts. First, answer part A. Then, answer part B.

Part A: What statement is true about the point of view of the passage?

A The passage is written from the first-person point of view.

B The passage is written from the third-person point of view.

C The point of view of the passage changes from first person to third person.

D There is not enough information to tell the point of view.

Part B: Which statement about the passage **best** helps you answer part A?

A The passage is based on events that could take place in real life.

B The passage has two main characters: the speaker and Liam.

C The passage uses words like I, me, and myself.

D The passage never uses words like I, me, and myself.

GO ON →

Read the passage. Then answer the questions.

Parties for Spring

When spring begins, Earth seems to wake up. The weather becomes warmer. There are more hours of sunlight each day. Trees grow green leaves and flowers bloom. Animals come out of their winter homes.

In spring, humans spend more time outside. Farmers start to work in their fields. People feel thankful that the dark, cold winter is over. People all over the world have celebrations, or parties, for the beginning of spring.

Holi

Holi (HOH-lee) is a celebration in northern India. India is a large country in Asia. Holi is the day before spring begins. Holi is a colorful day.

During Holi, people of all ages go into the streets. Then, the people throw powdered paint and colored water at each other. The people, streets, and buildings become covered in bright colors. The bright colors of the festival are like the bright colors of spring.

Nowruz

Nowruz (nou-ROOZ) is a New Year celebration. It is on the first day of spring. Nowruz started in the country of Iran. Iran is also in Asia.

GO ON →

On Nowruz, people get ready for the New Year. They might clean their homes, get haircuts, or buy new clothes. People eat special foods and visit each other. Adults give gifts. Children give flowers and desserts. It is a day for people to celebrate the New Year and the return of spring.

Spring Celebrations

There are spring celebrations in Mexico. Mexico is the country just south of the United States. On the first day of spring there are as many hours of daytime as of nighttime. This is special because it only happens twice a year.

People visit the pyramids in Mexico in spring.

In Mexico there are some very old cities. In one of these cities are some tall stone buildings called pyramids. On the first day of spring, people climb to the top. This lets them get closer to the sun. People feel that the sun gives them special energy on this first day of spring.

All around the world, people welcome spring. They are happy for the return of longer days and warmer weather.

GO ON →

Student Name _____

7 What is one thing that causes Earth to wake up in springtime?

    A bright colors

    B green leaves

    C people outside

    D warmer weather

8 Read the sentence from the passage.

People all over the world have <u>celebrations</u>, or parties, for the beginning of spring.

Which word from the sentence **best** helps you understand what <u>celebrations</u> means?

    A world

    B parties

    C beginning

    D spring

GO ON →

9   Read the sentence from the passage.

Holi is a <u>colorful</u> day.

Fill in the word web with words that mean the opposite of <u>colorful</u>. Choose **three** words from the word bank below.

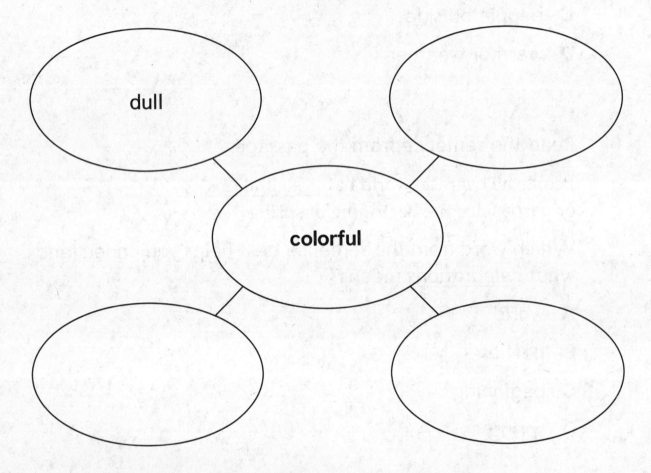

Word Bank		
bold	boring	bright
pale	plain	

GO ON →

10 This question has two parts. First, answer part A. Then, answer part B.

Part A: Why do people in Mexico climb to the top of a pyramid on the first day of spring?

A The people want to exercise their bodies.

B The people want to get as close as they can to the sun.

C The people want to have a good view of the land below.

D The people want to visit a very old place.

Part B: Which sentence from the passage **best** helps you answer part A?

A In Mexico, there are some very old cities.

B In one of these cities are some tall stone buildings called pyramids.

C On the first day of spring, people climb to the top.

D This lets them get closer to the sun.

GO ON →

11   Read the sentence from the passage.

The bright colors of the festival are like
the bright colors of spring.

Why does the author **most likely** compare the festival's
colors to the colors of spring?

A   to show that springtime looks different in different
parts of the world

B   to show why there are so many colors in springtime

C   to show how the colors of the festival are made

D   to show why special colors are used for the festival

GO ON →

Together

You used to be
My best friend.

We went everywhere
Together—
5   Up the stairs,
Down the slide,
Around the house.

We zoomed across the floors
Together—
10   Your engine roared
Like a lion
When I drove you.

We were always
Together—
15   Until you began to creek
And the paint on your wheels
Was gone.

What happened, my friend?
Did you get old or did I?

GO ON →

12 When the speaker of the poem says "you," who is the speaker talking to?

   A The speaker is talking to himself or herself.

   B The speaker is talking to Mom and Dad.

   C The speaker is talking to a toy car that was played with years ago.

   D The speaker is talking to another child from school.

13 Read lines 10 and 11 from the poem.

Your engine roared
Like a lion

Why does the speaker **most likely** compare an engine to a lion?

   A to show that it is funny

   B to show that it is noisy

   C to show that it is angry

   D to show that it is hungry

GO ON →

14 What is the theme of the poem?

    A Nothing lasts forever.

    B Learn from past mistakes.

    C Old friends are the best.

    D Promises should be kept.

15 What makes "Together" a free verse poem? Mark an X in the box next to **two** reasons.

	Free verse poem
It does not use rhyme.	☐
It tells about the speaker's feelings.	☐
It does not follow a set rhythm.	☐
It describes something from the past.	☐
It does not have stanzas.	☐

GO ON →

The draft below needs revision. Read the draft. Then answer the questions.

Bear in the Yard

(1) Zack heard a knock at the door, but he knew who it would be. (2) When he opened the door, his friend Alejandro was standing there with a backpack and a sleeping bag. (3) The boys was going to have a backyard campout!

(4) Alejandro followed Zack into the backyard. (5) When Alejandro seen the tent, he said, "Awesome!" (6) Zack helped Alejandro set up his sleeping bag.

(7) For a few hours, the boys enjoyed themselves in the tent. (8) They told stories. (9) They read books. (10) They imagined that they were camping in the mountains. (11) But then they heard a strange noise outside.

(12) "It sounds like a dangerous animal!" Alejandro whispered. (13) "Like a bear or something!"

(14) Zack knew there were'nt bears in his backyard, but the noise worried him. (15) An animal was definitely outside their tent, because he could hear it sniffing near the door.

(16) Then Zack remembered the walkie-talkie his mom have given him. (17) He called her, and the mystery was immediately solved. (18) There was a bear in the backyard. (19) It was Zack's big black dog named Bear! (20) Zack unzipped the tent, and Bear jumped in to spend the night with them.

GO ON →

16 What is the correct way to write sentence 3?

    A The boy's were going to have a backyard campout!

    B The boys were going to have a backyard campout!

    C The boys was going to have a backyard campout!

    D The boys is going to have a backyard campout!

17 What is the correct way to write sentence 5?

    A When Alejandro saw the tent, he said, "Awesome!"

    B When Alejandro seen the tent, he says, "Awesome!"

    C When Alejandro seen the tent, he said, Awesome!

    D When Alejandro saw the tent, he says, "Awesome!"

18 What is the **best** way to combine sentences 8 and 9?

    A They told stories and they read books.

    B They told stories, and read books.

    C They told stories and read books.

    D They told stories, they read books.

GO ON →

19   What is the correct way to write sentence 14?

   A   Zack know there weren't bears in his backyard, but the noise worried him.

   B   Zack knew there werent bears in his backyard, but the noise worried him.

   C   Zack knew there werent' bears in his backyard, but the noise worried him.

   D   Zack knew there weren't bears in his backyard, but the noise worried him.

20   What is the correct way to write sentence 16?

   A   Then Zack remembered the walkie-talkie his mom was given him.

   B   Then Zack remembered the walkie-talkie his Mom had given him.

   C   Then Zack remembered the walkie-talkie his mom had given him.

   D   Then Zack remembered the walkie-talkie his mom have given him.

GO ON →

Student Name _____

Answer these questions.

21   Which word begins with the same sound as <u>now</u>?

    A scent

    B crumb

    C knock

22   Which word has the same vowel sound as <u>dirt</u>?

    A worm

    B right

    C dart

23   Which word has the same vowel sound as <u>for</u>?

    A far

    B oar

    C hurt

GO ON →

Student Name _____

24 Which word has the same vowel sound as <u>cheer</u>?

    A dear

    B chirp

    C her

25 Which word has the same vowel sound as <u>wear</u>?

    A fear

    B wore

    C chair

Narrative Performance Task

Task:

Your class has been learning about how different environments make the world an interesting place. Your teacher has asked you to make up your own narrative, or story, to share what you've learned.

Before you decide what you will write about, you will read two passages, or sources, that provide information about different places plants and animals can live. After you have looked at these passages, or sources, you will answer some questions about them. Look at the passages and the three questions that follow. Then, go back and read the passages carefully. They will give you the information you will need to answer the questions, and write your own narrative, or story.

In Part 2, you will write your story using information from the two passages.

Directions for Part 1

You will now look at two passages, or sources. You can look at either of the passages as often as you like.

Research Questions:

After looking at the passages, use the rest of the time in Part 1 to answer three questions about them. Your answers to these questions will be scored. Also, your answers will help you think about the information you have read, which should help you write your story. You may look at the passages, or sources, when you think they would be helpful. You may also look at your notes.

GO ON →

Source #1: Inside a Pond

Did you know that most of the Earth is covered by water? Some of that water is freshwater. Freshwater is the water that we drink, wash with, and use to water plants. Ponds are made up of freshwater.

Ponds are all around us. They can be made by people or nature. Pond waters are mostly still and not very deep. In fact, sunlight can reach the bottom of a pond.

Ponds have plant and animal life. Pond plants and animals need each other to live. Animals need to live in safe places with food to eat.

The Pond's Food Chain

Every living thing needs energy. Plants get energy from the sun. Animals get energy from food. The food chain starts with plants. Plants grow with energy from the sun. Some animals get energy by eating plants, while other animals get energy by eating other animals.

Pond Plants

Many plants grow in and around ponds. Some plants, like irises, grow along the pond's edge. Their leaves and flowers grow above the ground, and their roots grow down into the ground. Other plants, like water lilies, grow in the pond. Their leaves and flowers float on top of the water, and their roots grow down into the pond's muddy bottom.

Pond plants help animals. Some animals use plants as hiding places. Other animals eat plants.

GO ON →

Pond Creatures

Many creatures live in ponds. Some insects and animals live on the water's surface. Creatures like insects live on top of the water. A pond skater is an insect that lives on top of the water. They have long legs. Their legs help them walk on water. Pond skaters eat other insects. Animals, like ducks, also live on the water's surface. Ducks eat plants and roots.

Some creatures live underwater. Fish and tadpoles live underwater. Fish eat plants and insects. Tadpoles are young frogs that eat small insects.

Crayfish and worms live on a pond's muddy bottom. Crayfish eat plants, dead fish, and insects. Worms eat mud and small bits of plants.

Bigger animals like raccoons and squirrels live near the pond. They drink water from the pond. Raccoons eat fish and plants found near the pond. Beavers eat plants found near the pond.

GO ON →

Source #2: Under the Ocean

Most of the Earth is covered by oceans. Oceans are made up of saltwater. Many kinds of plants and animals live in the ocean.

Oceans are very large and deep. The surface of an ocean is very large. Most oceans are larger than the surface of the United States. The average ocean is over 2.5 miles deep.

The plants and animals that live in oceans are called marine life. These plants and animals depend on each other to live. Marine plants use sunlight to make their own food. Marine animals cannot make their own food. Some marine animals, like fish and manatees, eat plants. Other marine animals, like turtles, eat plants and meat. Some marine animals, like penguins and sea lions, only eat meat. Plants help marine animals in other ways. Some marine animals hide behind plants.

The Ocean's Layers

An ocean is divided into three layers. The deeper you go in the ocean, the darker and colder it gets.

The top layer is called the sunlit zone. Sunlight enters this layer. This water is warmer since it gets sunlight. Sunlight gives plants the energy they need to grow. Some plants, like diatoms and seaweed, live here. Animals like sharks, seals, and sea lions live here too. More plants and animals live here than in the other zones.

GO ON →

The middle layer is called the twilight zone. These waters are poorly lit. The waters are much colder than in the sunlit zone. There is little light in this zone. Few plants live here. Most of the animals here eat meat. Animals, like the octopus, squid, and hatchet fish, live here.

The bottom layer is called the midnight zone. It is the darkest and deepest part of the ocean. No sunlight enters here. The waters are very cold. This layer has no plant life. There is little food. Few animals live in this zone. They have adapted to live here. Some animals have large mouths. Their mouths can catch any food that goes by. Fish, like the fangtooth and umbrellamouth gulper, can live here.

GO ON →

1   Pick **two** choices that show details about underwater plants or animals found in **both** "Inside a Pond" and "Under the Ocean."

   A Plants eat animals to give them energy.

   B Plants and animals can live underwater.

   C Marine plants and animals live in ponds.

   D Plants live along the bottom of the ocean.

   E Animals need plants in order to stay alive.

2   The sources discuss some of the plants and animals that live in ponds and oceans. Explain what you have learned about why plants are important for animals that live in ponds and oceans. Use **one** detail from **each** source to support your explanation.

   _____

   _____

   _____

   _____

   _____

GO ON →

Student Name _____

3 The sources explain that ponds and oceans have three different "layers." Why is this topic important? Use **one** example from **each** source to support your answer.

_____

_____

_____

_____

_____

GO ON →

Directions for Part 2

You will now look at your sources. You will take notes. Then, you will plan, draft, revise, and edit your story. First read your assignment and the information about how your story will be scored. Then begin your work.

Your Assignment:

Your class has been learning about different places plants and animals can live. Your assignment is to write a story that uses information about what you have learned about plants and animals that live in ponds and oceans.

Using information from the two sources, "Inside a Pond" and "Under the Ocean," write a story about a bird that visits a pond for a drink of water before flying to a nearby ocean. Write about what the bird sees other creatures, or animals, doing at the pond and ocean.

Your story must be several paragraphs long. Write the story from the point of view of the bird. Tell what the bird sees and does as it flies. Include information from both sources using your own words. Be sure to write who the story is about, where your story takes place, and what happens.

REMEMBER: A well-written story

- is well-organized and stays on the topic
- has an introduction and conclusion
- uses details from the sources
- develops ideas fully
- uses clear language
- follows rules of writing (spelling, punctuation, and grammar)

Now begin work on your story. Manage your time carefully so that you can plan, write, revise, and edit your story. Write your response on a separate sheet of paper.

Read the passage. Then answer the questions.

Abigail Adams

Birth and Youth

Abigail Smith was born on November 11, 1744, in Massachusetts. Her father worked in a church. Her mother was a part of the Quincy family. They were a respected family in the area.

Abigail did not go to school. But her mother taught her to read and write. As a child, Abigail read book after book in her family library. She learned about many different things. She also helped her mother in many ways. Together they often did charity work, helping people in need.

Marriage and Children

Abigail Smith and John Adams knew each other as children. But they met again as adults, and they were a good match. John liked Abigail's love of reading. He had spent many years in school, and now he was starting a law career. He asked Abigail to marry him. When they were married in 1764, Abigail Smith's name became Abigail Adams.

John and Abigail had six children. Sadly, not all of them lived to be adults. They lived on John's family farm in Massachusetts. John started to work in politics. He had to spend more time away from home. Abigail had to run the farm without him and also take care of the children by herself. She did well and helped the farm make money. But soon her husband's work led her down a different road.

GO ON →

Life in Politics

Beginning in 1778, John Adams was living in Paris much of the time, to do work there for the United States. In 1784, Abigail joined him there. Life in Paris was different and new for her. During this time, she learned how to run a different kind of household, living in a palace in a big city. She also learned how to take care of important guests from many countries.

The Adams family went back to the United States in 1788. In 1789, John became the first Vice President of the United States. Abigail did her best to help First Lady Martha Washington. For example, she helped her plan important dinners and parties. Abigail's time in Europe taught her about these matters.

In 1797, John Adams won the election to be the second President of the United States. Abigail became the country's second First Lady. In 1800, the Adams family moved into the new White House. They were the first family to ever live there. However, they did not live there for very long. In 1801, John lost his second election for president.

Later Life and Death

Abigail had troubles with her health for a while. This led her to spend as much time as possible at the family's home in Massachusetts. They called their home Quincy, after Abigail's mother's family. When John lost the election in 1801, he and Abigail moved back to Quincy for good.

GO ON →

In 1818, Abigail died of a disease called typhoid. Less than ten years later, her son John Quincy Adams became the sixth President of the United States. Abigail is buried at Quincy with two U.S. Presidents: her husband and her son.

Timeline

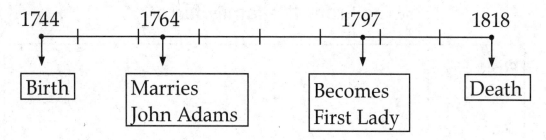

GO ON →

1 Read the events from the life of Abigail Adams. Then write each event in the chart in the correct order.

Abigail lives in the White House
Abigail marries John Adams.
Abigail learns how to read.
Abigail runs the family farm.

First . . .
Next . . .
Then . . .
Last . . .

GO ON →

2 Some words in the passage are in **bold print**. How do these words break the text apart?

    A They tell about the reasons Abigail Adams was important.

    B They tell about the people in Abigail Adams' family.

    C They tell about the places where Abigail Adams lived.

    D They tell about different times in Abigail Adams' life.

3 What did Abigail Adams do after she lived in Paris? Use **two** details from the passage in your answer.

_____

_____

_____

_____

_____

GO ON →

4   Read the sentence from the passage.

In 1797, John Adams won the <u>election</u> to be the second President of the United States.

What does the word <u>election</u> mean?

A   to choose someone for a job again

B   the act of choosing someone for a job

C   the opposite of choosing someone for a job

D   to choose more than one person for a job

5   What is the purpose of the timeline at the end of the passage?

A   The timeline helps readers keep track of the most important events in Adams' life.

B   The timeline shows readers where Adams lived at different times in her life.

C   The timeline shares information that cannot be shared in the passage.

D   The timeline lists the reasons that people think Adams was successful as First Lady.

GO ON →

Read the passage. Then answer the questions.

Making Dreams Come True

I have always dreamed about going camping in the woods. I've read stories about all the fun things you can do there. I imagine what I would see in the woods, and my mind is full of trees, flowers, and a shining sun. Then I start thinking about nighttime and a nice, warm campfire. Mom and Dad could help me roast marshmallows, and we could have hot chocolate. It all sounds perfect!

"Mom, can we take a trip to the woods?" I ask excitedly. "I really want to go camping. We could go hiking and maybe even see a waterfall!"

"That does sound delightful, but a trip like that takes planning," explains Mom. "We need to figure out where we want to go, where we can stay, and what we want to do. Also, we need to save a little extra money to help pay for the trip."

"Oh," I groan as I slump down in my seat. "That sounds like a lot of work. I was hoping we could go this weekend."

"Well, we can't go this weekend," says Mom, "but we can probably go next month. Why don't we start planning?"

My heart sinks. I don't want to wait a whole month. I want to go right away—the sooner, the better.

GO ON →

Mom hands me an enormous book of places to visit in our state. She flips to the section of state parks. Mom says I can pick where I would like to visit. There are so many pages that I feel like I will never be able to pick the right park. Luckily, there are lots of pictures to look at.

After what feels like hours, I pick a park. Mom agrees that it's a good choice, and I start to feel like the trip might happen soon. Then Mom reminds me we still have a lot of work to do, and the trip seems far away again.

Over the next few weeks, we plan our trip. First, we pick a place in the park where we will camp. Then, we choose what trails to hike on. Last, we find a waterfall nearby to visit. As we make each plan, the trip seems closer and closer!

I also try to help by making some extra money to spend on the trip. I rake leaves for my neighbors and feed my friends' cats when they are out of town. I put all of my money in a special jar, and each week the jar gets a bit fuller.

Before I know it, it is the night before the trip. I am so proud of my hard work that I can barely fall asleep. I know that when I wake up it will be time to go! As I drift to sleep, I smile because I know that my camping adventure is about to begin.

GO ON →

6 Who is telling the story?

    A a narrator who is part of the story

    B a narrator who is not part of the story

    C Mom

    D Dad

7 Read the sentence from the passage.

"That does sound <u>delightful</u>, but a trip like that takes planning," explains Mom.

The word <u>delight</u> means "happiness."
What does the word <u>delightful</u> in the passage tell that Mom thinks the trip will be?

    A happier than what happens before it

    B less happy than what happens after it

    C full of happiness

    D without happiness

GO ON →

8   Read the numbered definitions in the box below. Choose **two** correct meanings for <u>trip</u>, and write the numbers for those meanings in the word web.

Then read the sentence from the passage.

"Mom, can we take a <u>trip</u> to the woods?" I ask excitedly.

Mark an X in **one** box next to the meaning of <u>trip</u> used in the sentence.

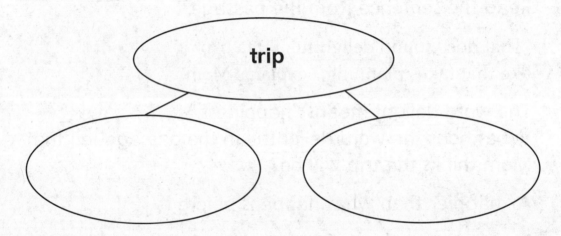

Definitions	
1 The act of falling, usually because of a bad step	☐
2 One part of an object that sticks out away from the rest	☐
3 An idea you tell someone, usually to help them	☐
4 A visit to another place	☐

GO ON →

9   What can you tell by reading the passage?

   A   what Mom and Dad want to pack for the trip

   B   what the narrator thinks about preparing for the trip

   C   what kind of trip the narrator wants to take next

   D   what Mom and Dad want to do on the trip

10   Read the sentence from the passage.

   Mom hands me an <u>enormous</u> book of places to visit in our state.

   What word means almost the same as <u>enormous</u>?

   A   empty

   B   large

   C   old

   D   soft

GO ON →

Read the passage. Then answer the questions.

Helping Build Homes

Have you heard of Habitat for Humanity? It is a group that thinks everyone should have a safe home. The word <u>Habitat</u> means "a place to live," and the word <u>Humanity</u> means "people." Many people do not have safe homes. Habitat fixes old homes and builds new homes for people who need them. Volunteers work for Habitat. Volunteers are people who choose to give their time without pay. Working for Habitat is a great experience that everyone should try.

Adults volunteer for Habitat. They help in many ways. Some volunteers help to fix old homes or build new homes. They learn many new skills. Others work at Habitat offices and stores to sell things in order to raise money. It can be hard work, but volunteers feel good knowing they are helping others.

Children volunteer for Habitat, too. They raise money through bake sales, car washes, and candy and flower sales. They also give their coins through a coin drive called "Nickels for Nails." Kids can also help out places where homes are being built. Kids can bring food to the workers at these places, or they can help plant flowers and trees.

GO ON →

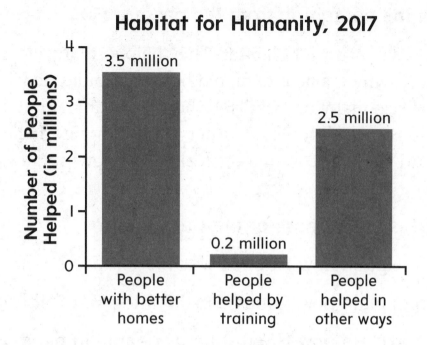

Habitat for Humanity, 2017

Why is it such a great idea to volunteer for Habitat? The answer is simple. Working for Habitat teaches you why it is important to help others. It also teaches you helpful skills that you can use in other parts of your life. You may learn how to build something. You may learn how to make your home more Earth-friendly.

Best of all, Habitat teaches children how to work together toward a shared goal. At Habitat, you learn that people can make a big difference in the lives of others. That is why everyone should consider working for Habitat.

GO ON →

11   Read the paragraph from the passage.

Adults volunteer for Habitat. They help in many ways.
Some volunteers help to fix old homes or build new homes.
They learn many new skills. Others work at Habitat offices
and stores to sell things in order to raise money. It can
be hard work, but volunteers feel good knowing they are
helping others

What is the purpose of this paragraph?

A   to explain how Habitat was first created

B   to explain how adults can volunteer for Habitat

C   to explain how Habitat helps people in need

D   to explain how children can volunteer for Habitat

12   Read the sentence from the passage.

Best of all, Habitat teaches children how
to work together toward a shared goal.

**Which words mean the same as the word goal?
Choose two.**

A   aim

B   start

C   end

D   beginning

E   ball

GO ON →

13 Read the sentence from the passage.

They also give their coins through a coin drive called "Nickels for Nails."

Then read the dictionary entry.

---

drive \drīv\ *noun*

1. a trip in a car **2.** a project in which people work together to raise money **3.** in science, a need in the body to act in a given way **4.** in golf, a strong hit with a club

---

Which meaning of the word <u>drive</u> is used in the sentence?

A meaning 1

B meaning 2

C meaning 3

D meaning 4

14 What does the bar graph in the passage help the reader understand?

   A what people who volunteer for Habitat should expect

   B which skills people needed to volunteer for Habitat in 2017

   C why Habitat helped people find safe homes in 2017

   D how many people Habitat helped in different ways in 2017

GO ON →

15 The following question has two parts. First, answer part A. Then, answer part B.

Part A: Why did the author **most likely** write this passage?

A to tell where the reader can volunteer for Habitat

B to show what types of houses Habitat has built

C to explain the history of Habitat

D to get the reader to volunteer for Habitat

Part B: Which sentence from the passage **best** helps you answer part A?

A Volunteers are people who choose to give their time without pay.

B Working for Habitat is a great experience that everyone should try.

C Some volunteers help to fix old homes or build new homes.

D You may learn how to make your home more Earth-friendly.

GO ON →

The draft below needs revision. Read the draft. Then answer the questions.

Amelia Earhart

(1) Amelia Earhart was a great pilot. (2) She was born in Kansas on July 24 1897. (3) She saw her first plane when she was ten, but she did'nt think it was too interesting. (4) But when she rode with a pilot in 1920, she knew she had to fly.

(5) Soon after, she started taking flying lessons. (6) She saved and borrowed money to buy their own plane. (7) She started setting flying records. (8) She was invited to make a special flight. (9) She would be the first woman to fly across the Atlantic ocean.

(10) At about age 40, she tried to be the first woman to fly around the world. (11) Sadly, she and her plane was lost in the Pacific Ocean. (12) Even today, no one knows what happened to her.

GO ON →

16 What is the correct way to write sentence 2?

    A She was born in kansas on July 24, 1897.

    B She was born in Kansas on July, 24 1897.

    C She was born in Kansas on July 24, 1897.

    D She was born in Kansas on, July 24, 1897.

17 What is the correct way to write sentence 3?

    A She saw his first plane when she was ten, but she didn't think it was too interesting.

    B She saw her first plane when she was ten, but she didnt think it was too interesting.

    C She saw her first plane when she was ten, but she did'nt think it was too interesting.

    D She saw her first plane when she was ten, but she didn't think it was too interesting.

GO ON →

18 What is the **best** way to write sentence 6?

    A She saved, and borrowed money to buy their own plane.

    B She saved and borrowed money to buy her own plane.

    C She saved and borrowed money to buy their own plane.

    D She saved and borrowed money to buy my own plane.

19 What is the correct way to write sentence 9?

    A She would be the first woman to fly across the Atlantic Ocean.

    B She would be the first women to fly across the Atlantic Ocean.

    C She would be the first woman to fly across the Atlantic ocean.

    D She would be the first woman to fly across the atlantic Ocean.

20 What is the **best** way to write sentence 11?

    A Sadly, she and her plane was lost in the Pacific Ocean.

    B Sadly, her and her plane were lost in the Pacific Ocean.

    C Sadly, she and her plane were lost in the Pacific Ocean.

    D Sadly, she and her plane was lost in the Pacific ocean.

GO ON →

Student Name _____

Answer these questions.

21 Which word has the same vowel sound as <u>out</u>?

    A poor

    B cow

    C oil

22 Which word has the same vowel sound as <u>joy</u>?

    A choice

    B judge

    C jaw

23 Which word has the same vowel sound as <u>spoon</u>?

    A ought

    B spoil

    C fruit

GO ON →

Student Name _____

24 Which word has the same vowel sound as <u>caught</u>?

  A could

  B catch

  C thought

25 Which word has the same vowel sound as <u>egg</u>?

  A weather

  B myth

  C touch

Informational Performance Task

Task:

Your class has been learning about how people can make a difference. Your teacher has asked you to write an informational article about how people can make a difference.

Before you decide what to write about, you will read two passages, or sources, that provide information about paramedics and about the American Red Cross. After you have looked at these passages, or sources, you will answer some questions about them. Look at the passages and the three questions that follow. Then, go back and read the passages carefully. They will give you the information you will need to answer the questions and write an informative article.

In Part 2, you will write an informational article using information from the two passages.

Directions for Part 1

You will now look at two passages, or sources. You can look at either of the passages as often as you like.

Research Questions:

After looking at the passages, use the rest of the time in Part 1 to answer three questions about them. Your answers to these questions will be scored. Also, your answers will help you think about the information you have read, which should help you write your informational article. You may look at the passages, or sources, when you think they would be helpful. You may also look at your notes.

GO ON →

Source #1: Help from Paramedics

Sometimes something important or dangerous happens very fast, so people must act immediately. This is called an emergency.

Paramedics are people who help others. They take care of people who have accidents, such as falling down. They help people who suddenly get sick. Paramedics quickly treat the sick or hurt person and take the person to a hospital. At the hospital, doctors work to cure the person.

How do paramedics find the sick or hurt person? When someone suddenly gets hurt or sick, a family member or friend makes an emergency phone call to 911. The 911 worker calls the paramedics.

To get to the hurt or sick person, the paramedics drive an ambulance. This is a special kind of car or van that is used to carry people who are hurt or sick. An ambulance holds special machines and supplies.

The paramedics must get to the person right away. They must take the person to the hospital quickly, too. That is why an ambulance has special markings and a siren. A siren makes a loud sound to warn other cars. Cars pull over to let the ambulance go by. The ambulance driver must be very careful when driving.

Paramedics work in teams of two. One paramedic drives the ambulance. The other paramedic rides in the back, helping the person. Together they bring the person to the hospital. At the hospital, the team tells a doctor what happened and the doctor takes over.

GO ON →

When paramedics are helping someone, they can get help, too. A paramedic can call a doctor, and the doctor can tell the paramedic what to do.

To become paramedics, people must study and train. They work long and hard. They spend many months in classes taught by doctors. They must learn how to tell what is wrong with a sick or hurt person. They must learn how to use equipment. Paramedics practice their skills. This helps them learn how to do their job. The training and practice make them ready to help people.

Paramedics must make sure that the ambulance is always clean. They must put supplies in the ambulance. They check the ambulance after they take care of each sick or hurt person. Then they get another call from 911. They head off to help the next person.

Paramedics are part of a large team that help people who get hurt or sick. They are usually the first ones to give aid. Paramedics are very important emergency workers in a community!

GO ON →

Source #2: Help from the Red Cross

The American Red Cross helps people in many ways. They help people when there are accidents or emergencies. The Red Cross helps soldiers and their families. They teach safety classes. The Red Cross also works with volunteers in other countries.

Many people can be hurt by disasters, or sudden events that cause a lot of loss. There are many kinds of disasters. Disasters can be small like house fires. A house fire might only involve one family. Disasters can be large like hurricanes. A hurricane could involve a team of workers helping thousands of families. The Red Cross gives people food, medical care, and a place to stay after disasters.

Disasters and emergencies can happen in any community at any time. Workers and volunteers are ready to travel to wherever they are needed. They might work long hours at a time. They work in teams to help people who are hungry, sick, or homeless.

The American Red Cross helps those in the armed forces. Life can be hard for soldiers and their families. The Red Cross helps soldiers who have been hurt. The Red Cross helps soldiers and their families stay in touch. They also help the families who are away from their loved ones.

GO ON →

The Red Cross teaches safety classes in many communities. They teach first-aid classes for adults and children. There are classes that teach children to swim and about water safety. Teenagers and adults can learn how to be lifeguards. The Red Cross even teaches children to become careful babysitters.

The American Red Cross also works with volunteers from other countries. They help with disasters and emergencies in other parts of the world. They also work to keep people in other countries safe.

Volunteers make up a large part of the American Red Cross. People can give their time and their skills to help others in an emergency. People can give blood to help those who might need it when they are in a hospital. People can give money to help buy ambulances and supplies. Children can volunteer at hospitals, take babysitter safety training, or write letters to soldiers. All of these people help the Red Cross to help others in need.

GO ON →

Student Name _____

1 Which information about how people can make a difference are found in **both** "Help from Paramedics" and "Help from the Red Cross"? Pick **two** choices.

  A Workers work in teams.

  B Children can help paramedics.

  C People hurt by emergencies need help.

  D Soldiers cannot get help from children.

  E Volunteers can help in many ways.

2 "Help from Paramedics" and "Help from the Red Cross" tell about some ways helpers act in emergencies. Write a paragraph about what you have learned about how people can help others. Use **at least one** detail from **each** source in your answer.

_____

_____

_____

_____

_____

GO ON →

3   Write a paragraph about how teams work together to
    help make a difference. In your answer, use **at least one**
    detail from "Help from Paramedics" and **at least one**
    detail from "Help from the Red Cross."

    _____

    _____

    _____

    _____

    _____

GO ON →

Directions for Part 2

You will now look at your passages, or sources. You will take notes. Then, you will plan, draft, revise, and edit your article. First read your assignment and the information about how your informational article will be scored. Then begin your work.

Your Assignment:

Your class has been learning about how people can make a difference. Your assignment is to write an informational article that uses information about what you have learned about paramedics and about the American Red Cross.

Use information from the two sources, "Help from Paramedics" and "Help from the Red Cross," for your article. In your article, tell how the helpers in these sources are alike and how they are different.

Your article must be several paragraphs long. Make sure to have a main idea. Support your main idea with details from the sources. Remember to use your own words. Be sure to state your ideas clearly.

REMEMBER: A well-written informational article

- has a clear main idea
- is well-organized and stays on the topic
- has an introduction and conclusion
- uses transitions
- uses details from the sources to support your main idea
- develops ideas fully
- uses clear language
- follows rules of writing (spelling, punctuation, and grammar)

Now begin work on your informational article. Manage your time carefully so that you can plan, write, revise, and edit your article. Write your response on a separate sheet of paper.

STOP

Read the passage. Then answer the questions.

Saving Shipwrecked Sailors

A warm summer day at the beach is fun, but when a storm hits, the sea can be full of danger. The coast of Cape Cod, Massachusetts, is one place that is less dangerous than it used to be. For years, there were many shipwrecks, and then lifesaving stations were built.

In 1872, nine lifesaving stations were built on Cape Cod. The stations were wooden buildings that were painted red. The bright color helped sailors on ships see them. Stations were right on the beach, close to the sea, and a lookout tower was part of each station.

A crew of six people worked at each station. Their job was to rescue the sailors on ships that were sinking.

All the crew members were good with boats. They got special training to learn lifesaving skills and how to use new equipment. The crews practiced what to do in an emergency, and they timed their practices and always tried to work faster.

The crews looked for ships in trouble in two ways. One way was by watching from the beach. Every night, two crew members walked on the beach and looked out to sea. The other way was by watching from the lookout tower at the station. Crew members took turns as lookouts high up in the tower, where they could see far out to sea.

GO ON →

Crew members watched for ships in trouble from the lookout tower.

Sometimes the crew members on the beach saw a ship, and sometimes the crew members in the tower saw one. When a ship needed help, the crew was ready to act at the drop of a hat. Quickly, they headed out to the ship. They went in small boats, called surfboats, and brought the sailors safely to shore. The crew members had to work fast, and their training and practice helped them be quick.

Then things changed. In the 1900s, stronger ships were built that were less likely to sink. Also, people could predict the weather better, so ships were not caught in storms.

The lifesaving stations are no longer needed. Most of them are gone today, but the Old Harbor Lifesaving Station remains. The U.S. National Park Service keeps it open for visitors. During the summer, park rangers act out a rescue once a week.

GO ON →

1 The following question has two parts. First, answer part A. Then, answer part B.

Part A: Read the paragraph from the passage.

A <u>crew</u> of six people worked at each station. Their job was to rescue the sailors on ships that were sinking.

What does the word <u>crew</u> mean in the paragraph?

A part of a boat

B group of workers

C type of sport

D kind of job

Part B: Which words from the paragraph **best** help you answer part A?

A of six people

B at each station

C rescue the sailors

D were sinking

GO ON →

Student Name _____

2 Which sentence from the passage states **both** the problem and the solution?

   A For years, there were many shipwrecks, and then lifesaving stations were built.

   B Stations were right on the beach, close to the sea, and a lookout tower was part of each station.

   C Crew members took turns as lookouts high up in the tower, where they could see far out to sea.

   D Sometimes the crew members on the beach saw a ship, and sometimes the crew members in the tower saw one.

3 What are some of the problems with the ships that needed to be solved? Use **two** details from the passage in your answer.

_____

_____

_____

_____

_____

GO ON →

4 Read the sentence from the passage.

When a ship needed help, the crew was ready to act <u>at the drop of a hat</u>.

What do the words <u>at the drop of a hat</u> mean?

A The crew members would help at night.

B The crew members would help when they got a signal.

C The crew members would help right away.

D The crew members would help after they got their gear.

5 Read the paragraph from the passage.

The lifesaving stations are no longer needed. Most of them are gone today, but the Old Harbor Lifesaving Station <u>remains</u>. The U.S. National Park Service keeps it open for visitors. During the summer, park rangers act out a rescue once a week.

Which word in the paragraph **best** helps to show the meaning of <u>remains</u>?

A stations

B gone

C summer

D rescue

GO ON →

Read the play. Then answer the questions.

The Husband and Wife

Characters
HUSBAND
WIFE
STRANGER
ZEUS

[*Setting: A small, plain hut at the top of a hill. A village lies at the bottom of the hill.*]

NARRATOR: The villagers were cooking a huge dinner for a visit from Zeus. A husband and wife lived in the hut at the top of the hill. They had only what they needed and not much extra. To make the feast for Zeus, they had been saving their food for days.

HUSBAND: [*Yelling into the hut*] My dear wife! Two strangers are coming up the hill. They look hungry, thirsty, and tired.

WIFE: [*From inside the hut*] They must not have found help in the village. They can eat and rest here. Surely Zeus will understand.

STRANGER: [*To the husband*] We have been traveling for a long time, and we are very hungry. Everyone in the village below turned us away. Will you help us?

HUSBAND: Of course, you are welcome in our home! The more, the merrier! [*Leads the stranger and his friend into the hut*]

WIFE: [*To the stranger and his friend*] Welcome to our home! Please, sit down and eat of this feast.

Copyright © McGraw-Hill Education

GO ON →

NARRATOR: The husband and wife gave the strangers all the food they had cooked for Zeus. Unlike their neighbors in the village below, they showed kindness to the travelers. As their guests ate, the husband and wife noticed something strange. The food never ran out. The drink never ran out. It was as if their guests had some kind of magic. . . .

WIFE: [*To her husband quietly*] These are no ordinary guests.

HUSBAND *nods.*

NARRATOR: At bedtime, the husband and wife slept on the floor so their guests could sleep on the bed. In the morning, the strangers prepared to leave.

STRANGER: Thank you again for your kindness. [*A bright, golden light suddenly floods the stranger's face. For a moment, his face is the sun.*]

HUSBAND: [*Wide-eyed and amazed*] What strange wonder is this?!

WIFE: It is Zeus himself! [*Both the husband and the wife bow deeply.*] We are honored to have you as a guest. You are the star that guides us, great one!

ZEUS: You have one wish. Whatever you wish for shall be yours.

HUSBAND AND WIFE: [*Together*] Please allow us to stay together for the rest of our lives!

ZEUS: Granted. This wish and more is now yours.

NARRATOR: When the couple turned back to their hut, it had become a grand castle. The couple turned back to thank Zeus, but both travelers had disappeared. The couple lived in the castle for many more years together. Until one day when they were very, very old . . .

GO ON →

HUSBAND: The end of our lives is near. I wish we could live forever together.

WIFE: [*Taking husband's hand*] So do I, my dear husband.

NARRATOR: And the next day, everything had disappeared from the top of the hill except for two trees. Today those trees still stand side by side. When the wind blows through its leaves, one tree whispers, "My dear husband." And the other tree replies, "My dear wife."

GO ON →

6 Read the sentence from the play.

The more, the merrier!

What does this sentence show about the husband?

A He thinks his home is too small for guests.

B He welcomes guests to his home.

C He does not often have guests at his home.

D He wants the guests to never leave.

7 Read the sentence from the play.

For a moment, his face is the sun.

What does comparing Zeus's face to the sun show about Zeus?

A Zeus is dangerous.

B Zeus is very warm.

C Zeus is embarrassed.

D Zeus is full of magic.

GO ON →

8   Why are the stage directions in the play important?

    A   They show which characters are in the play.

    B   They show how the play's secret is shown onstage.

    C   They show when the play is coming to an end.

    D   They show what the characters say to each other.

9   The following question has two parts. First, answer part A. Then, answer part B.

    Part A: Why does the wife compare Zeus to a star?

    A   to show that Zeus lives far away

    B   to show that Zeus belongs up in the sky

    C   to show that Zeus is someone she and her husband follow

    D   to show that Zeus can be dangerous if he comes into their house

    Part B: Which sentence from the play **best** helps you answer part A?

    A   Surely Zeus will understand.

    B   Welcome to our home!

    C   These are no ordinary guests.

    D   We are honored to have you as a guest.

GO ON →

10 Read the sentences in the box. Circle **two** sentences that state a theme from the play.

Be careful when trusting a stranger.

Change can be both good and bad.

Show kindness and you will be rewarded.

True love can find a way to last.

Difficult tasks are easier with teamwork.

---

11 How would the play be different if Zeus were telling it?

   A Zeus would travel to the village alone.

   B The villagers would welcome Zeus and be kind to him.

   C The reader would always know Zeus is one of the strangers.

   D The husband and wife would turn Zeus away.

GO ON →

Read the poem. Then answer the questions.

They Didn't Think
by Phoebe Cary

Once a trap was baited
With a piece of cheese;
It tickled so a little mouse,
It almost made him sneeze.

5   An old rat said, "There's danger,
Be careful where you go!"
"Nonsense!" said the other,
"I don't think you know!"
So he walked in boldly—

10   Nobody in sight—
First he took a nibble,
Then he took a bite;
Close the trap together
Snapped as quick as wink,

15   Catching mousey fast there,
'Cause he didn't think.
Once there was a robin,
Lived outside the door,
Who wanted to go inside

GO ON →

20   And hop upon the floor.
"No, no," said the mother,
"You must stay with me;
Little birds are safest
Sitting in a tree."

25   "I don't care," said Robin,
And gave his tail a fling,
"I don't think the old folks
Know quite everything."
Down he flew, and kitty seized him

30   Before he'd time to blink;
"Oh," he cried, "I'm sorry,
But I didn't think."

"They Didn't Think" by Phoebe Cary from *Poems Every Child Should Know*. Doubleday, Doran & Co., Inc. 1904.

GO ON →

12 Which line **best** tells the message of the poem?

   A It almost made him sneeze.

   B First he took a nibble,

   C "No, no," said the mother,

   D But I didn't think."

13 What do the stanzas of the poem tell about?

   A the same character in different situations

   B different characters who make the same mistake

   C two different endings

   D two of the same settings

14 Which two lines in the poem rhyme?

   A lines 6 and 8

   B lines 7 and 9

   C lines 15 and 16

   D lines 27 and 28

GO ON →

15 What is the point of view of each character in the poem? Mark an X in **one** box for **each** character.

	Point of View: Be careful	Point of View: Do not worry
Little mouse	☐	☐
Old rat	☐	☐
Mother	☐	☐
Robin	☐	☐

GO ON →

The draft below needs revision. Read the draft. Then answer the questions.

Jumping Spiders

(1) Jumping spiders have many things in common with other spiders, but they are also different in a few ways.

(2) Like all spiders, jumping spiders have two main body parts and eight legs. (3) Some jumping spiders have hairy bodies, and some have bright colors about their mouths.

(4) Like other spiders, most jumping spiders usually live alone in an web, which they build under leaves or in another safe place. (5) Some spiders will use their sticky web to catch prey, but jumping spiders use their webs only for a safe rest.

(6) Jumping spiders' eyes are huge and work gooder than other spiders' eyes, helping them see clearly over far distances. (7) Jumping spiders need to have excellent vision so they are able to catch their prey.

(8) Jumping spiders get their names because they usually jump on their prey to catch them. (9) For example, if a jumping spider sees a grasshopper on a leaf, it will jump on the grasshopper and bite it? (10) The spider might jump so quickly and from such a distance that the grasshopper doesnt know it's there until it's too late!

GO ON →

16 What is the **best** way to write sentence 3?

    A Some jumping spiders have hairy bodies, but some have bright colors about their mouths.

    B Some jumping spiders have hairy bodies, and some have bright colors around their mouths.

    C Some jumping spiders have hairy bodys, and some have bright colors about their mouths.

    D Some jumping spiders have hairy bodies, and some have bright colors to their mouths.

17 What is the correct way to write sentence 4?

    A Like other spiders, most jumping spiders usualy live alone in an web, which they build under leaves or in another safe place.

    B Like other spiders, most jumping spiders usually live alone in a web, which they build under leaves or in another safe place.

    C Like other spiders, most jumping spiders usually live alone in an web, which they build under leaves or in another save place.

    D Like other spiders, most jumping spiders usually live alone in a web, which they build under a leaves or in another safe place.

GO ON →

18 What is the correct way to write sentence 6?

    A Jumping spiders' eyes is huge and work gooder than other spiders' eyes, helping them see clearly over far distances.

    B Jumping spiders' eyes are huge and work gooder then other spiders' eyes, helping them see clearly over far distances.

    C Jumping spiders' eyes are huge and work better than other spiders' eyes, helping them see clearly over far distances.

    D Jumping spiders' eyes are huger and work better than other spiders' eyes, helping them see clearly over far distances.

19 What is the correct way to write sentence 9?

    A for example, if a jumping spider sees a grasshopper on a leaf, it will jump on the grasshopper and bite it.

    B For example, if a jumping spider sees a grasshopper on a leaf, it will jump on the grasshopper and bite it?

    C For example, if a jumping spider sees a grasshopper on a leave, it will jump on the grasshopper and bite it?

    D For example, if a jumping spider sees a grasshopper on a leaf, it will jump on the grasshopper and bite it.

GO ON →

20 What is the **best** way to write sentence 10?

A The spider might jump so quickly and from such a distance that the grasshopper doesnt know it's there until it's to late!

B The spider might jump so quickly and from such a distance that, the grasshopper doesnt know it's there until it's too late!

C The spider might jump so quickly and from such a distance that the grasshopper doesn't know it's there until it's too late!

D The spider's might jump so quickly and from such a distance that the grasshopper doesn't know it's there until it's too late!

GO ON →

Student Name _____

Answer these questions.

21 Which word has **two** closed syllables?

    A kitten

    B human

    C lady

22 Which word has a CVC*e* syllable?

    A music

    B napkin

    C describe

23 Which word ends with the same syllable sound as <u>shuttle</u>?

    A grateful

    B mental

    C lately

GO ON →

Student Name _____

24 Which vowel teams help you read the word <u>moonbeam</u>?

A on, am

B oo, ea

C mo, nb

25 Which word has the same vowel sound in the **first** syllable as <u>circus</u>?

A counter

B silver

C turtle

Opinion Performance Task

Task:

Your class has been learning about how our world works. Your teacher has asked you to write an opinion article about which is a better way to learn about Earth's oceans, by exploring from a submarine or exploring from a boat.

Before you decide what you will write about, you will read two passages, or sources, that provide information about Earth's oceans. After you have looked at these passages, or sources, you will answer some questions about them. Look at the passages and the three questions that follow. Then, go back and read the passages carefully. They will give you the information you will need to answer the questions and write an opinion article.

In Part 2, you will write an opinion article using information from the two passages.

Directions for Part 1

You will now look at two passages, or sources. You can look at either of the passages as often as you like.

Research Questions:

After looking at the passages, use the rest of the time in Part 1 to answer three questions about them. Your answers to these questions will be scored. Also, your answers will help you think about the information you have read, which should help you write your opinion article. You may look at the passages, or sources, when you think they would be helpful. You may also look at your notes.

GO ON →

Source #1: Under the Deep Sea

People have always thought about the bottom of Earth's oceans. People swam down into the dark ocean waters. They hoped to see living things. They wanted to go as far down as possible. But they could not go very deep. They needed air to breathe. They needed a ship to take them there.

In 1580, a man named William Bourne had an idea. He thought that a ship could be built to go underwater and come back up again. Forty years later, Cornelius Drebbel built the first working submarine. A submarine is a ship that can carry people underwater. This special ship helps people breathe air while underwater. It lets people take a trip under the sea.

Today underwater explorers still travel in submarines. The submarines use things like cameras and computers. Some even have robots that can leave the submarine. The robots may gather pieces from the ocean floor. These pieces help scientists learn more about the Earth. The explorers also take pictures and movies of the living things that they see. The pictures can be studied long after the submarine comes out of the water.

A submarine gets ready to explore the underwater world.

Purestock/SuperStock

Copyright © McGraw-Hill Education

GO ON →

The deepest known underwater place on Earth is called Challenger Deep. It is in the Pacific Ocean very far from the US. It was found by some sailors over one hundred years ago. In 1960 two men traveled to the bottom of Challenger Deep in a submarine. The trip down took five hours. When they got to the bottom, the water was very cloudy. They were not able to get clear pictures of Challenger Deep. The explorers had to go back up before the water cleared.

Other scientists have made the trip to Challenger Deep. In 2012, a man named James Cameron went down in a submarine. Cameron had worked with other people to build a special submarine. It was only large enough to carry one person. Cameron's trip to Challenger Deep was made into a movie. Now other people would be able to see the deepest place on Earth.

Another way that a submarine can be used is to find sunken ships. In 1985 a submarine called Argo was used to find a famous ship, the Titanic. The ship had sunk in 1912 as it made its first trip across the Atlantic Ocean. A sea explorer named Robert Ballard dreamed of finding the Titanic. Using Argo, Ballard found the large ship. His dream came true.

Since over half of Earth is under water, exploring it all will take many years. The job is as large as the oceans!

GO ON →

Source #2: Gifts of the Ocean

The beautiful oceans of Earth have given people many gifts. These large bodies of water are filled with living and nonliving things. They make our lives better. Scientists are finding new ways to use these gifts.

Ocean waters are home to fish and shellfish. People have eaten fish for thousands of years. Shellfish such as shrimp and lobsters have also been eaten by many people. Fish can also be used in other ways. The oil found in the bodies of some fish can be used in items like shampoo and medicine. Some shellfish give us very special gifts. Pearls which are formed inside of oysters are used to make rings, necklaces, and other jewelry.

**Pearls form inside of an oyster.
They are shiny and strong.**

Plants are very important. They make oxygen for the Earth. Oxygen is the gas that we need to breathe. Oceans cover about 70% of the Earth. That means that most of the oxygen is made by plants in the oceans.

Ocean plants help us in other ways. Some ocean plants can be used for food. Some soups and salads contain seaweed. Other ocean plants are used to make medicines. Still other ocean plants are used in such products as toothpaste, sunscreen, and pet food.

GO ON →

lynx/iconotec.com/Glow Images

Ocean water is not the same as fresh water. It contains salt. The salt makes it taste very different. Scientists have found ways to take the salt out of sea water. The water can then be used for drinking. The salt can be used for cooking. This helps people who live where there is not a lot of fresh water to drink.

The oceans provide ways for people to travel. Large boats carry items between places that are very far apart. People also travel on the oceans for fun. Boat rides on the ocean can give people the chance to see animals that they have never seen. Whales and dolphins might be seen as people ride through the ocean waves. Some people enjoy sailing on the ocean as well.

Oceans give us a beautiful place to visit and have fun. Surfers ride the waves. Divers go underwater to look at living things. Families enjoy digging in the sand. People may collect shells on the beach. Swimming in the salty ocean is enjoyed by many people.

Scientists have already found one million kinds of plants and animals living in the oceans. There may be millions of other plants and animals that have not yet been discovered. We have no idea how many gifts are still hidden in the oceans of Earth!

GO ON →

Student Name _____

1   Which details explain what **both** "Under the Deep Sea"
    and "Gifts of the Ocean" say about Earth's oceans? Pick
    two choices.

    A   Many people are interested in the Earth's oceans.

    B   The oceans on Earth have been **completely** explored.

    C   Life in the ocean is nearly the same as life on the land.

    D   The living things found in Earth's oceans can help
        people.

    E   People can best enjoy the oceans by going to the
        deepest parts.

2   Look at the pictures and captions from "Under the Deep
    Sea" and "Gifts of the Ocean." How do they help you
    better understand the information about Earth's oceans?
    For **each** picture and caption, include **one** way it helps
    you to better understand Earth's oceans.

    _____

    _____

    _____

    _____

    _____

    _____

GO ON →

3 Explain what the world would be like if people could not explore the oceans by boat or by submarine. Use **one** detail from "Under the Deep Sea" and **one** detail from "Gifts of the Ocean" to support your answer. For **each** detail, include the source name or number.

_____

_____

_____

_____

_____

_____

GO ON →

Directions for Part 2

You will now look at your passages, or sources. You will take notes. Then, you will plan, draft, revise, and edit your opinion article. First read your assignment and the information about how your opinion article will be scored. Then begin your work.

Your Assignment:

Your class has been learning about how our world works. Your teacher wants everyone in class to write an opinion article about which is the better way of exploring the Earth's oceans, by submarine or by boat.

Use information from the two sources, "Under the Deep Sea" and "Gifts of the Ocean," to support your opinion article. In your article, state and support your opinion about which way of exploring you think is better.

Your article must be several paragraphs long. Make sure to give a clear opinion. Support your opinion with details from the sources. Remember to use your own words. Be sure to state your ideas clearly.

REMEMBER: A well-written opinion article

- has a clear opinion
- is well-organized and stays on the topic
- has an introduction and conclusion
- uses transitions
- uses details from the sources to support your opinion
- develops ideas fully
- uses clear language
- follows rules of writing (spelling, punctuation, and grammar)

Now begin work on your opinion article. Manage your time carefully so that you can plan, write, revise, and edit your article. Write your response on a separate sheet of paper.

Unit 1 Answer Key

Student Name: _____

Question	Correct Answer	Content Focus	Complexity
1A	D	Character	DOK 2
1B	B	Character/Text Evidence	DOK 2
2	C	Character	DOK 1
3	C, D	Text Features: Illustrations	DOK 2
4	see below	Root Words with -ed, -ing	DOK 1
5	A	Key Details	DOK 1
6	see below	Setting	DOK 1
7	A	Synonyms	DOK 1
8	B, D	Root Words with -ed, -ing	DOK 1
9A	C	Key Details	DOK 1
9B	D	Key Details/Text Evidence	DOK 1
10	see below	Key Details	DOK 3
11	B, D	Synonyms	DOK 1
12	C	Synonyms	DOK 2
13	A	Text Features: Charts	DOK 2
14	see below	Root Words with -ed, -ing	DOK 1
15	A	Text Features: Illustrations	DOK 1
16	A	Sentence Capitalization	DOK 1
17	B	Quotation Marks with Dialogue	DOK 1
18	C	Combining Sentences	DOK 2
19	D	Expanding Sentences	DOK 2
20	C	Sentence Punctuation	DOK 1
21	B	Short a	DOK 1
22	C	Short e	DOK 1
23	C	Two-Letter Blends	DOK 1
24	B	Long a	DOK 1
25	C	Long i	DOK 1

Unit 1 Answer Key

Student Name: _____

Comprehension 1A, 1B, 2, 3, 5, 6, 9A, 9B, 10, 13, 15	/18	%
Vocabulary 4, 7, 8, 11, 12, 14	/12	%
English Language Conventions 16, 17, 18, 19, 20	/5	%
Phonics 21, 22, 23, 24, 25	/5	%
Total Unit 1 Assessment Score	/40	%

4 Students should circle the following words:
- adding
- adds

6 Students should match the following:
- Beginning of story – Rico's home
- Middle of story – the store
- End of story – Rico's home

10 **2-point response:** Students should explain that "the friend who likes the jam best is Chipmunk" and that Chipmunk wants to "make up for all the jam" he has eaten at Rabbit's house, so Chipmunk must like jam.

14 Students should complete the chart with the following:
- grow + ing = <u>growing</u>
- call + <u>ed</u> = called
- <u>drink</u> + ing = drinking

Unit 1 Answer Key

Student Name: _____

Narrative Performance Task			
Question	**Answer**	**Complexity**	**Score**
1	B, E	DOK 3	/1
2	see below	DOK 3	/2
3	see below	DOK 3	/2
Story	see below	DOK 4	/4 [P/O] /4 [D/E] /2 [C]
Total Score			**/15**

2 **2-point response:** Animals help people in many ways. "Service Dogs" tells about dogs who can help people who cannot do things for themselves. Dogs can help their owners walk or warn them if there is danger. "Helping Each Other" tells about horses who can carry people, dogs who can rescue people in a storm, and pets who can keep people from being lonely.

3 **2-point response:** Animals and people can help each other in different and important ways. "Service Dogs" tells how dogs can become part of a family. A dog can help the family members, and the family cares for and feeds the dog. "Helping Each Other" tells more about people and animals helping each other. Eve Fertig helps animals, and she teaches others how to do it, too. Her own dog, Shana, dug a tunnel to rescue Eve in a storm.

10-point anchor paper: My father told me that I do not spend enough time outside. He told me to think about something that I would like to do outdoors. I thought about soccer or basketball. I thought I could have fun playing either one, but I couldn't decide which to try.

Then one day, on my way home from school, I walked past the animal shelter. At the animal shelter, dogs and cats wait for people to adopt them and take them home. When I walked by, I saw boys and girls walking dogs on leashes. It looked like fun. Suddenly, I could not wait to get home and talk to my dad. I wanted to tell him that I had found something to do outdoors.

When I got home, my dad asked if I had picked soccer or basketball. "Neither," I said. "I found something even better." I explained that I wanted to help out at the animal shelter by walking dogs. My dad loved my idea. He wanted to help out too.

Later, we went to the shelter to sign up. A nice man told us that they needed more help on Wednesday afternoons. We signed up. Each Wednesday, we walked over to the shelter together. We clipped leashes onto the collars of the dogs we were going to walk. Some dogs got so excited they started barking and hopping around. We took them on long walks in the neighborhood.

I got to know all the different dogs in the shelter. I liked them all, but my favorite was Tramp, a fuzzy little dog with white fur. He liked sniffing new things on our walks. I wished that I could take him home with me. One day after school, my dad asked me, "Are you ready for a walk?" I was confused because it was Thursday. My dad handed me a brand new leash. I had no idea what was going on. Just then, Tramp ran into the room and stopped right in front of me. I gasped in surprise. I bent down to pet him and I saw that he had a new collar. Hanging from it was a shiny dog tag that said "Tramp" and our phone number.

Now, I walk every day. On Wednesdays, I walk the dogs at the animal shelter. On the other days, I walk with Tramp. He is my best friend.

Unit 1 Rationales

1A

A is incorrect because although the passage states that Mama was very busy all week, this does not show that she is kind.

B is incorrect because Mama does not let Rico cook alone.

C is incorrect because although Mama does drive Rico to the store, this does not show that she is kind.

D is correct because Mama shows kindness by welcoming her new neighbors.

1B

A is incorrect because this sentence does not tell about Mama.

B is correct because this sentence shows that it was kind of Mama to invite the new neighbors to dinner.

C is incorrect because although this sentence is said by Mama, it shows that she is knows that there is still work to do and does not show that Mama is kind.

D is incorrect because although this sentence is said by Mama, it shows that she is knows that there is still work to do and does not show that Mama is kind.

2

A is incorrect because Mama asked the new neighbors to dinner, so she knows who is coming.

B is incorrect because the passage indicates that Mama is worried for a different reason.

C is correct because the passage explains that "Mama was very busy all week" and the dinner is at the end of this busy week.

D is incorrect because there are no details in the passage that support this idea.

3

A is incorrect because although this might be true and the illustration shows Rico, it does not show him eating tacos.

B is incorrect because although this might be true and the illustration shows Rico, it does not show him with friends.

C is correct because the illustration shows Rico cleaning tomatoes.

D is correct because the illustration shows Rico working at the kitchen sink.

E is incorrect because although the illustration shows Rico, it does not show him writing a shopping list.

4

The words *adding* and *adds* are correct because they have the same root word as *added*.

The words *address, admit,* and *adventure* are incorrect because they do not have the same root word as *added*.

5

A is correct because Mama and Rico each got a few items at the same time, so they spent less time shopping,

B is incorrect because Mama and Rico had the same items on the grocery list no matter how they shopped for them.

C is incorrect because Mama and Rico were not racing or playing a game.

D is incorrect because the way Mama and Rico gathered the food does not change the number of items they needed to buy.

6

The correct answers are "Rico's home," "the store," and "Rico's home." The action in the story begins and ends at Rico and Mama's home, but in the middle, Rico and Mama go to the store.

7

A is correct because the words *keep* and *last* are synonyms.

B is incorrect because the word *next* is not a synonym for the word *last*.

C is incorrect because the word *end* is not a synonym for the word *last* in this sentence.

D is incorrect because the word *quit* is not a synonym for the word *last*.

8

A is incorrect because the word *look* is used here as a command, not a past-tense verb ending in *-ed*.

B is correct because the word *picked* is a past-tense verb ending in *-ed*, so it shows an action that happened in the past

C is incorrect because the word *first* is used here as an adjective, not a past-tense verb ending in *-ed*.

D is correct because the word *filled* is a past-tense verb ending in *-ed*, so it shows an action that happened in the past

E is incorrect because the word *many* is used here as an adjective, not a past-tense verb ending in *-ed*.

9A

A is incorrect because Rabbit knows that his mom makes jam, so this does not surprise him on Jam Day.

B is incorrect because Rabbit knows that the jam lasts all year, so this does not surprise him on Jam Day.

C is correct because after stating that Chipmunk picked blackberries very fast, the passage states "Rabbit is surprised."

D is incorrect because although Rabbit may have been surprised that Dad was silent, the passage does not indicate this.

9B

A is incorrect because this sentence tells about making jam but does not tell about what surprises Rabbit.

B is incorrect because this sentence tells about eating jam but does not tell about what surprises Rabbit.

C is incorrect because although this sentence is about how Chipmunk is picking blackberries, the question is asked by Rabbit's dad and does not tell about Rabbit.

D is correct because this sentence is said by Rabbit and expresses his surprise about Chipmunk picking blackberries.

10

See answer key for sample response.

11

A is incorrect because the word *loud* is not a synonym for the word *silent*.

B is correct because the words *still* and *silent* are synonyms.

C is incorrect because the word *upset* is not a synonym for the word *silent*.

D is correct because the words *quiet* and *silent* are synonyms.

E is incorrect because the word *happy* is not a synonym for the word *silent*.

12

A is incorrect because the word *alone* is not a synonym for the word *tiny*.

B is incorrect because the word *safe* is not a synonym for the word *tiny*.

C is correct because the words *small* and *tiny* are synonyms.

D is incorrect because the word *under* is not a synonym for the word *tiny*.

13

A is correct because the elephant newborn is the largest of the animals included in the chart.

B is incorrect because the chart presents only the animals' weights at birth, not their heights.

C is incorrect because the chart does not indicate the number of animal babies born at a time.

D is incorrect because the animals in this chart are large both as babies and as adults.

14

The new word *growing* is correct because it correctly combines the root word *grow* with the inflectional ending *-ing*.

The inflectional ending *-ed* is correct because if added to the root word *call*, it will make the new word *called*.

The root word *drink* is correct because it is the root word to which the inflectional ending *-ing* can be added to form the new word *drinking*.

15

A is correct because the illustration shows a baby hippo with its mother.

B is incorrect because the illustration shows only one mother hippo with her baby.

C is incorrect because the illustration does not show a hippo drinking milk.

D is incorrect because the illustration does not show a hippo drinking under the water.

16

A is correct because every sentence must begin with a capital letter.

B is incorrect because the sentence should begin with a capital letter and because a second comma is not needed in this sentence.

C is incorrect because the sentence should begin with a capital letter and because a proper noun such as a person's name should begin with a capital letter.

D is incorrect because the sentence should begin with a capital letter and end with a period, since it is not a question.

17

A is incorrect because quotation marks are needed to call out the dialogue in the sentence.

B is correct because the quotation is set off correctly with quotation marks put in the correct places.

C is incorrect because the opening quotation mark is placed too early and does not mark where the dialogue begins.

D is incorrect because the closing quotation mark is placed too early and does not mark where the dialogue ends.

18

A is incorrect because the sentence does not combine the common idea in both sentences and instead repeats the idea.

B is incorrect because although the sentence combines the common idea in the sentences, it uses an incorrect conjunction

C is correct because the sentence combines the common idea in the two sentences by using the conjunction *and* to form a compound subject.

D is incorrect because the sentence does not combine the common idea in both sentences and it uses an incorrect conjunction.

19

A is incorrect because it incorrectly indicates an incorrect cause-and-effect relationship between the details.

B is incorrect because it indicates an incorrect sequence of events and also indicates an incorrect cause-and-effect relationship between the details.

C is incorrect because it indicates an incorrect sequence of events.

D is correct because it indicates the correct sequence of events and does not indicate any cause-and-effect relationship between the details.

20

A is incorrect because a comma is needed to set off a direct quotation from the rest of a sentence.

B is incorrect because *birthday* is not a proper noun or a part of a title here, so it should be lowercase.

C is correct because this sentence from Mom is clearly full of enthusiasm and excitement, so it is an exclamation and should end with an exclamation point.

D is incorrect because all direct quotations should begin and end with a quotation mark to show the exact words said.

21

A is incorrect because the word *cake* has a long *a* sound rather than a short *a* sound.

B is correct because the word *tap* has a short *a* sound.

C is incorrect because the word *tape* has a long *a* sound rather than a short *a* sound.

22

A is incorrect because the word *bean* has a long *e* sound rather than a short *e* sound.

B is incorrect because the word *bee* has a long *e* sound rather than a short *e* sound.

C is correct because the word *beg* has a short *e* sound.

23

A is incorrect because the word *rim* does not have a two-letter blend.

B is incorrect because the word *tip* does not have a two-letter blend.

C is correct because the word *tree* has the same two-letter blend as the word *trip*.

24

A is incorrect because the word *bad* has a short *a* sound rather than a long *a* sound.

B is correct because the word *name* has a long *a* sound.

C is incorrect because the word *mad* has a short *a* sound rather than a long *a* sound.

25

A is incorrect because the word *it* has a short *i* sound rather than a long *i* sound.

B is incorrect because the word *pin* has a short *i* sound rather than a long *i* sound.

C is correct because the word *time* has a long *i* sound.

Unit 2 Answer Key   Student Name: _____

Question	Correct Answer	Content Focus	Complexity
1	B	Main Topic and Key Details	DOK 2
2	D	Homographs	DOK 1
3	see below	Antonyms	DOK 2
4	see below	Main Topic and Key Details	DOK 1
5	C	Suffixes -*ly*, -*y*	DOK 1
6A	C	Main Topic and Key Details	DOK 2
6B	D	Main Topic and Key Details/Text Evidence	DOK 2
7A	D	Character, Setting, Plot: Problem and Solution	DOK 2
7B	C	Character, Setting, Plot: Problem and Solution/Text Evidence	DOK 2
8	C, E	Antonyms	DOK 2
9	see below	Story Structure: Beginning, Middle, End	DOK 2
10	B	Suffixes -*ly*, -*y*	DOK 1
11	B	Key Details	DOK 1
12	see below	Rhyme	DOK 1
13	A	Homographs	DOK 1
14	C	Key Details	DOK 1
15	A	Visual Patterns and Structure	DOK 2
16	B	Plural Nouns with -*es*	DOK 1
17	D	Apostrophes: Contractions	DOK 1
18	A	Capitalization of Proper Nouns	DOK 1
19	D	Commas in a Series	DOK 1
20	C	Irregular Plural Nouns	DOK 1
21	C	Long *o*	DOK 1
22	A	Long *u*	DOK 1

Copyright © McGraw-Hill Education

Student Name: _____

Question	Correct Answer	Content Focus	Complexity
23	B	Soft *g*	DOK 1
24	B	Consonant Digraphs and Trigraphs	DOK 1
25	C	Three-Letter Blends	DOK 1

Comprehension 1, 4, 6A, 6B, 7A, 7B, 9, 11, 12, 14, 15	/18	%
Vocabulary 2, 3, 5, 8, 10, 13	/12	%
English Language Conventions 16, 17, 18, 19, 20	/5	%
Phonics 21, 22, 23, 24, 25	/5	%
Total Unit 2 Assessment Score	/40	%

3 Students should match the following antonyms:
- first — last
- far — near
- came — went
- pull — push

4 **2-point response:** Students should mention two of the following details from the passage that describe how kites have helped people: Kites have been used to help people send messages; catch fish; build bridges; pull wagons, boats, and sleds; learn about weather; see very far away; call for help.

9 Students should match the following:
- Beginning: The wolf goes to see the crane.
- Middle: The crane helps the wolf.
- End: The crane learns a lesson.

12 Students should circle the following words:
- night
- bright

Unit 2 Answer Key   Student Name: _____

Informational Performance Task			
Question	Answer	Complexity	Score
1	A, C	DOK 3	/1
2	see below	DOK 3	/2
3	see below	DOK 3	/2
Informational Article	see below	DOK 4	/4 [P/O] /4 [E/E] /2 [C]
Total Score			/15

2 **2-point response:** "A Horse of a Different Color" says that baby zebras are called foals. They are white with brown stripes that later turn black. Baby zebras know their mothers by their stripes, and they can run when they are only one hour old. "Giraffes" says that baby giraffes can run when they are ten hours old. Baby giraffes are called calves.

3 **2-point response:** The patterns on the coats of zebras and giraffes are one thing that help keep them safe from their enemies. Zebra stripes make them look blurry when they run. Giraffe spots help them blend in with trees. These things make it hard for their enemies to see zebras and giraffes.

10-point anchor paper: Zebras and giraffes are interesting animals. They are alike in some ways and different in others. In the past people thought that zebras and giraffes were mixtures of different animals.

Zebras and giraffes live in Africa. Zebras live in family groups. Many zebra families form a large herd with hundreds of zebras. Giraffes live in herds too. Giraffe herds are much smaller than zebra herds.

Zebras and giraffes both have patterned coats. No zebra or giraffe has the exact same pattern to their coat. A zebra's coat is white with black stripes. A giraffe's coat is white or tan with spots. Giraffes are much taller than zebras. Zebras look like horses. Giraffes are so tall they can see into a second-floor window.

Both zebras and giraffes have babies. Baby zebras are foals. Baby giraffes are calves. Baby zebras and giraffes can walk soon after birth. Baby zebras can walk 20 minutes after birth. Baby giraffes can walk less than an hour after they are born. Baby zebras and giraffes can run when they are less than a day old. Baby zebras can run when they are an hour old. Baby giraffes can run when they are 10 hours old.

Africa can be a dangerous place for zebras and giraffes to live. Both animals have enemies. Lions and wild dogs are zebras' enemies. Giraffes' enemies are lions and crocodiles. Zebras and giraffes have coats that help keep them safe from their enemies. Zebras and giraffes kick their legs to fight their enemies.

Zebras and giraffes are both alike and different.

Unit 2 Rationales

1

A is incorrect because this sentence is an introduction to the topic before the main idea is presented.

B is correct because this sentence sums up the main idea that all the paragraphs support.

C is incorrect because this sentence states the main idea of the second paragraph only, not the main topic of the entire passage.

D is incorrect because this sentence is a supporting detail in the second paragraph.

2

A is incorrect because the word *line* is not used in this sentence to mean a line drawn on paper.

B is incorrect because the word *line* is not used in this sentence to mean a line or edge that is crossed over.

C is incorrect because the word *line* is not used in this sentence to mean a line that people wait in.

D is correct because the word *line* is used in this sentence to mean a thin string used to catch fish.

3

The adjectives *first* and *last* are antonyms. The adjectives *far* and *near* are antonyms. The verbs *came* and *went* are antonyms. The verbs *pull* and *push* are antonyms.

4

See answer key for sample response.

5

A is incorrect because the suffix *-y* in the word *lucky* does not mean "not caring about."

B is incorrect because the suffix *-y* in the word *lucky* does not mean "without."

C is correct because the suffix *-y* means "having," indicating that *lucky* means "having good luck."

D is incorrect because the suffix *-y* in the word *lucky* does not mean "in need of."

6A

A is incorrect because the main idea of the paragraph is not about the size of the kites built long ago.

B is incorrect because although the paragraph is partly about Alexander Graham Bell, the main idea expands on this detail to include the role of kites in the invention of the airplane.

C is correct because it includes all the details and information in the paragraph.

D is incorrect because although the paragraph is partly about the Wright Brothers studying birds, this is only one detail in the paragraph.

6B

A is incorrect because it focuses on only the first detail of the paragraph and does not support the main idea.

B is incorrect because it focuses on only one detail and does not support the main idea of the paragraph.

C is incorrect because it focuses on only one detail and does not support the main idea of the paragraph.

D is correct because this sentence summarizes the main idea that kites were used by those who invented the airplane.

7A

A is incorrect because the first paragraph in the passage explains that the wolf is eating.

B is incorrect because the third paragraph explains that the wolf finds the crane at the river.

C is incorrect because the next to last paragraph explains that the wolf does not intend to give the crane a reward.

D is correct because it states the wolf's problem: a bone is stuck in the wolf's throat, so he cannot continue eating.

7B

A is incorrect because this sentence tells what the crane usually does when she sees the wolf, not what she does to solve the wolf's problem.

B is incorrect because this sentence tells what the crane does right before she solves the wolf's problem.

C is correct because this sentence tells that the crane pulls the bone out of the wolf's throat, thus solving his problem.

D is incorrect because this sentence tells what the crane thinks after she solves the wolf's problem.

8

A is incorrect because the word *old* is not an antonym of the word *large*.

B is incorrect because the word *cold* is not an antonym of the word *large*.

C is correct because the words *small* and *large* are antonyms.

D is incorrect because the word *hard* is not an antonym of the word *large*.

E is correct because the words *tiny* and *large* are antonyms.

9

At the beginning of the passage, the wolf goes to see the crane to ask her to remove the bone that is stuck in his throat. In the middle of the passage, the crane helps the wolf by using her beak to pull the bone out of his throat. At the end of the passage, the crane learns the lesson that she cannot trust the wolf because he is a bad, mean animal.

10

A is incorrect because the suffix *-ly* in the word *proudly* does not mean "not."

B is correct because the suffix *-ly* in the word *proudly* shows that the crane danced "in a proud way."

C is incorrect because the suffix *-ly* in the word *proudly* does not mean "again."

D is incorrect because the suffix *-ly* in the word *proudly* does not mean "one who is."

11

A is incorrect because the details in the poem describe the speaker looking up at something in the night sky, not flying through the night sky.

B is correct because the poem describes the speaker looking up at a "steel gray bird" gliding slowly in the night sky.

C is incorrect because the "steel gray bird," not the speaker, has a beam "that shines so bright."

D is incorrect because although it is night, the speaker is looking up at the sky and not dreaming.

12

The only two words that rhyme from these lines are *night* and *bright*.

13

A is correct because the speaker uses the word *watch* to say that the speaker looks at the plane in the sky.

B is incorrect because the speaker does not use the word *watch* to mean "a clock that is worn on the wrist."

C is incorrect because the speaker does not use the word *watch* to mean "a period of time in which to wait."

D is incorrect because the speaker does not use the word *watch* to mean "a set time when something is done."

14

A is incorrect because although flying to the moon would require an education, the speaker never mentions school.

B is incorrect because although clouds are commonly located in the sky where airplanes fly, the speaker never mentions clouds.

C is correct because the details at the end of the poem indicate that the speaker wants to "touch the Moon."

D is incorrect because the speaker does not mention wanting to visit Mars.

15

A is correct because the structure of the poem helps show that the speaker sees an airplane in the sky.

B is incorrect because the image of the airplane formed by the structure of the poem does not indicate which words rhyme in the poem.

C is incorrect because the image of the airplane formed by the structure of the poem does not indicate when the poem was written.

D is incorrect because the image of the airplane formed by the structure of the poem does not indicate who the speaker is.

16

A is incorrect because the correct plural form of *bench* is spelled *benches.*

B is correct because the correct plural form of *bench* is *benches.*

C is incorrect because the plural form of *bench* is a common noun and should not be capitalized.

D is incorrect because although the correct plural form of *bench* is *benches,* the first word in the sentence should be capitalized.

17

A is incorrect because the word *It's* is a contraction in this sentence, not a possessive pronoun, so it should have an apostrophe.

B is incorrect because the contraction *It's* should have the apostrophe placed where the letter *i* in the word *is* has been left out.

C is incorrect because the contraction *It's* should have the apostrophe placed where the letter *i* in the word *is* has been left out.

D is correct because the word *It's* is correctly written to show the contraction for "It is."

18

A is correct because Sunday is a day of the week, a proper noun, so the word *Sundays* should be capitalized.

B is incorrect because the word *everyone* is a common noun and should not be capitalized.

C is incorrect because the singular form of *pond* is correct in this sentence.

D is incorrect because the word *Sundays* is a proper noun and should be capitalized.

19

A is incorrect because the comma placed before the beginning of the series is incorrect and because commas are needed in the list of animals.

B is incorrect because additional commas are needed to separate the animals in the series.

C is incorrect because the comma placed after the word *and* is incorrect and because commas are needed to separate the animals in the series.

D is correct because the commas correctly separate each animal in the series.

20

A is incorrect because the word *year* is a common noun in this sentence and should not be capitalized and because the sentence has an incorrect form of the irregular plural noun *mice.*

B is incorrect because the word *baby* is an adjective in this sentence, so it should not have a plural ending, even though it modifies a plural noun.

C is correct because the word *mouse* has an irregular plural form: *mice.*

D is incorrect because the sentence has an incorrect form of the irregular plural noun.

21

A is incorrect because the word *rock* has a short *o* sound rather than a long *o* sound.

B is incorrect because the word *hop* has a short *o* sound rather than a long *o* sound.

C is correct because the word *drove* has a long *o* sound.

22

A is correct because the word *mule* has a long *u* sound.

B is incorrect because the word *cut* has a short *u* sound rather than a long *u* sound.

C is incorrect because the word *rut* has a short *u* sound rather than a long *u* sound.

23

A is incorrect because although the word *led* has the same first three letters as the word *ledge*, it has a different end sound.

B is correct because the word *cage* has the same soft *g* end sound as the word *ledge*.

C is incorrect because although the word *gem* has a soft *g* beginning sound, it has a different end sound than the word *ledge*.

24

A is incorrect because although the word *wit* has the same first three letters as the word *witch*, it has a different end sound.

B is correct because the word *watch* has the same /ch/ end sound as the word *witch*.

C is incorrect because the word *wash* has a /sh/ end sound rather than a /ch/ end sound.

25

A is incorrect because although the word *spring* has the same ending two-letter digraph as the word *strong*, it has a different beginning three-letter blend.

B is incorrect because although the word *wrong* has a sequence of the same three letters as the word *strong*, those letters are not a three-letter blend.

C is correct because the word *strict* begins with the same three-letter blend as the word *strong*.

Unit 3 Answer Key

Student Name: _____

Question	Correct Answer	Content Focus	Complexity
1A	D	Main Idea and Key Details	DOK 2
1B	B	Main Idea and Key Details/Text Evidence	DOK 2
2	A	Prefixes *re-, dis-*	DOK 1
3	see below	Synonyms	DOK 2
4	A	Author's Purpose	DOK 2
5	C	Prefixes *re-, dis-*	DOK 1
6	see below	Plot: Sequence	DOK 1
7	B	Synonyms	DOK 2
8	see below	Plot: Sequence	DOK 1
9	D	Compound Words	DOK 1
10	see below	Main Idea and Key Details	DOK 1
11	A	Text Features: Heads (Subheads)	DOK 1
12	D	Compound Words	DOK 1
13	C	Text Features: Graphs	DOK 1
14	D	Text Features: Graphic Features (Diagrams)	DOK 2
15	A, E	Author's Purpose	DOK 2
16	C	Sentence Punctuation	DOK 1
17	A	Subject-Verb Agreement	DOK 1
18	D	Commas in a Series	DOK 1
19	C	The Verb *Have*	DOK 1
20	B	Present-, Past-, and Future-Tense Verbs	DOK 1
21	B	Long *a*	DOK 1
22	C	Long *i*	DOK 1
23	A	Long *o*	DOK 1
24	B	Long *e*	DOK 1
25	C	Long *u*	DOK 1

Comprehension 1A, 1B, 4, 6, 8, 10, 11, 13, 14, 15	/18	%
Vocabulary 2, 3, 5, 7, 9, 12	/12	%
English Language Conventions 16, 17, 18, 19, 20	/5	%
Phonics 21, 22, 23, 24, 25.	/5	%
Total Unit 3 Assessment Score	/40	%

3   Students should match the word *survive* with the words *continue* and *live*.

6   Students should mark an X for each event to show the following sequence:

- 1: Noor waits for Harriet to get off the truck.
- 2: Noor begins to ride around the block on Harriet.
- 3: Noor sees Mr. Paz in his garden.
- 4: Noor offers to carry plants in Harriet's basket.

8   **2-point response:** Students should include two of the following details in their answer: Noor's sister is excited about her new bedroom. Noor thinks about her old neighborhood. Noor was feeling sad. Noor had to blink back her tears. Noor checked to see if her bicycle had been unloaded from the truck.

10   Students should match the following:

- How do animals help the saguaro? – The animals spread saguaro seeds.
- How does the saguaro help animals? – The animals eat the saguaro fruit.

Opinion Performance Task			
Question	**Answer**	**Complexity**	**Score**
1	B, D	DOK 3	/1
2	see below	DOK 3	/2
3	see below	DOK 3	/2
Opinion Article	see below	DOK 4	/4 [P/O] /4 [E/E] /2 [C]
Total Score			**/15**

2   **2-point response:** "The Mail is Here!" tells that, before there was a postal service, people had to work very hard to share news with family and friends by asking others to carry their letters. "Bell's Telephone" says that Alexander Graham Bell worked hard to help people share their news by sending messages over an electrical wire. When the telephone was invented, people all over the world wanted to own one.

3   **2-point response:** From Source #1, I know that if the United States Postal Service had not been formed, people would have to drive around to take their mail or find a person to take it for them. The source says that after post offices were opened, people could take their letters and packages there to be delivered by the post office workers. Source #2 lets me know that if the telephone had not been invented, people would not be able to make calls. This might mean that people could not talk to others unless they were in the same place.

10-point anchor paper: These sources tell about the invention of two ways that people can share news with others—by mail and by telephone. The service that I think is more important is the telephone. There are many reasons why I believe telephones are more important than the mail service.

First, telephones allow us to hear the voice of the person we call. If your dad is away on a trip, hearing his voice makes you feel like he is not as far away. Also, hearing someone's voice lets me know how they are feeling more than words written in a letter.

Another reason that I believe that telephones are more important than the mail service is you can share news right away. For example, suppose you are having a birthday party and the guests are coming soon. If you suddenly get sick with the flu, there is no time to mail letters telling the guests not to come. The telephone lets your family call guests quickly so that they know that the party has been called off.

Finally, telephones are more important than the mail service because you can talk to people wherever you are. Cell phones let us call people even when we are away from home. Letters are delivered to your house, so you have to be at home to get them. That makes sharing news more difficult.

Although both the mail service and telephones are good ways to share news with others, I am most happy that I have telephone service. It helps me hear the voices of the people I am talking with, it is quick, and I can get and share the news wherever I am.

Unit 3 Rationales

1A

A is incorrect because this is a detail that supports the main idea of the passage.

B is incorrect because this is a minor detail included at the end of the passage.

C is incorrect because this is a minor detail that supports the main idea of the passage.

D is correct because the passage explains how people moved Rocketi from a wildlife center to an animal park and then to the San Diego Zoo to help her survive.

1B

A is incorrect because this sentence gives a detail about the ideas in only the first two paragraphs.

B is correct because this sentence tells about workers wanting to help Rocketi to survive

C is incorrect because this sentence is only a supporting detail about the San Diego Zoo.

D is incorrect because although this sentence is about how Rocketi feels about humans, the sentence is only a supporting detail.

2

A is correct because the prefix *dis-* means "not" or "the opposite of."

B is incorrect because the prefix *dis-* does not mean "wrongly."

C is incorrect because the prefix *dis-* does not mean "someone who."

D is incorrect because the prefix *dis-* does not mean "again."

3

The words *continue* and *live* are correct because they have similar meanings to the word *survive*; there are clues in the third paragraph of the passage to support these options. The words *grow, eat,* and *play* are incorrect because they do not have similar meanings to the word *survive*.

4

A is correct because the author describes the life of a cheetah cub named Rocketi throughout the entire passage.

B is incorrect because the author only briefly mentions the San Diego Zoo.

C is incorrect because the author only refers to raising a cheetah cub in relation to Rocketi.

D is incorrect because the author only mentions animal ambassadors in the context of Rocketi.

5

A is incorrect because the prefix *re-* does not mean "not."

B is incorrect because the prefix *re-* does not mean "before."

C is correct because the prefix *re-* means "again."

D is incorrect because the prefix *re-* does not mean "able to."

6

The passage begins with Noor waiting for Harriet to be unloaded from the truck. Once she receives the bike, Noor begins to ride Harriet around the block. While riding Harriet, she sees Mr. Paz in his garden and stops to talk to him. She learns that he needs help carrying plants, so she offers to carry them in Harriet's basket.

7

A is incorrect because the word *lifted* is not a synonym for the word *grinned*.

B is correct because the words *smiled* and *grinned* are synonyms.

C is incorrect because the word *stood* is not a synonym for the word *grinned*.

D is incorrect because the word *went* is not a synonym for the word *grinned*.

8

See answer key for sample response.

9

A is incorrect because although the words *watched, moving,* and *unload* all are made up of a root word combined with a prefix or inflectional ending, the sentence does not contain any compound words.

B is incorrect because although the past-tense verb *pumped* is made up of the word *pump* and the inflectional ending *-ed,* the sentence does not contain any compound words.

C is incorrect because although the words *squeezed* and *stopped* are both past-tense verbs with the inflectional ending *-ed,* the sentence does not contain any compound words.

D is correct because the compound word *handlebars* is formed by combining the words *handle* and *bars*.

10

Animals help the saguaro by spreading its seeds and giving it the opportunity to continue to grow in places throughout the desert. The saguaro helps animals by providing fruit for them to eat.

11

A is correct because this section of the passage describes the purposes and functions of the saguaro's strong roots, which help keep it upright in strong desert winds.

B is incorrect because this section of the passage tells how tall a saguaro grows and how its seeds get planted.

C is incorrect because this section of the passage tells about Saguaro National Park in Arizona.

D is incorrect because this section of the passage tells how people try to protect the saguaro with microchips.

12

A is incorrect because the word *workers* consists of the root word *work* with the suffix *-er* and the plural inflectional ending *-s.*

B is incorrect because the word *protect* does not consist of two smaller words.

C is incorrect because the word *adopted* consists of the root word *adopt* with the inflectional ending *-ed.*

D is correct because the compound word *someone* consists of the words *some* and *one*.

13

A is incorrect because the graph does not necessarily show the maximum age that the oldest saguaro reached.

B is incorrect because the graph does not necessarily show the tallest saguaro alive today.

C is correct because the graph shows the correlation between the age and height of a saguaro.

D is incorrect because the diagram does not necessarily show the maximum height a saguaro can grow to.

14

A is incorrect because the diagram does not show the microchip and the saguaro drawn to scale.

B is incorrect because the diagram does not show that a microchip can store facts.

C is incorrect because the diagram does not show where a microchip is bought.

D is correct because the diagram shows a picture of a microchip.

15

A is correct because the author informs the reader of facts about saguaros.

B is incorrect because, although the author mentions that it is possible to adopt a saguaro, the author does not attempt to encourage the reader to adopt a saguaro.

C is incorrect because the author only briefly mentions the fact that President Hoover set aside land for saguaros.

D is incorrect because the author does not argue that the saguaro is the best cactus.

E is correct because the author informs the reader about how people help protect saguaros.

16

A is incorrect because the first word of a sentence should be capitalized.

B is incorrect because the Corn Palace is a singular noun, not a plural noun, so the verb must also be singular, and because the sentence is a question, not a statement.

C is correct because the sentence is a question, not a statement.

D is incorrect because the sentence has a punctuation error.

17

A is correct because the subject of the verb is *rainbow*, which is a singular noun, so the singular form of the verb is required.

B is incorrect because *rainbow* is not a proper noun and because the singular form of the verb is needed to agree with the singular noun *rainbow*.

C is incorrect because *corn* is not part of a proper noun in this sentence.

D is incorrect because the sentence has a subject-verb agreement error.

18

A is incorrect because commas are needed to separate the colors in the sentence.

B is incorrect because a comma should not be placed after the word *and* in the sentence.

C is incorrect because a comma should not be placed after the word *had* and because commas are needed to separate all the colors in the sentence.

D is correct because the commas are placed correctly to separate the three colors in the sentence.

19

A is incorrect because *Dad* is a proper noun here and is also the first word of the sentence.

B is incorrect because the subject of the verb is the plural noun *murals,* so the plural form of the verb is required.

C is correct because the subject of the verb is the plural noun *murals,* so the plural form of the verb is required.

D is incorrect because the sentence is a statement, not a question, and because the subject of the verb is the plural noun *murals,* so the plural form of the verb is required.

20

A is incorrect because the pronoun that correctly agrees with the pronoun *us* later in the sentence is *we,* not *they.*

B is correct because the verbs are consistent and are both in the past tense.

C is incorrect because *Dad* is used as a proper noun in this sentence and should be capitalized and because for consistency the verbs should both be in the past tense, not the future tense.

D is incorrect because the sentence is a statement, not a question.

21

A is incorrect because the word *ran* has a short *a* sound rather than a long *a* sound.

B is correct because the words *weigh* and *rain* both have a long *a* sound.

C is incorrect because the word *graph* has a short *a* sound rather than a long *a* sound.

22

A is incorrect because the word *me* has a long *e* sound rather than a long *i* sound.

B is incorrect because the word *may* has a long *a* sound rather than a long *i* sound.

C is correct because the words *might* and *my* both have a long *i* sound.

23

A is correct because the words *slow* and *so* both have a long *o* sound.

B is incorrect because the word *stop* has a short *o* sound rather than a long *o* sound.

C is incorrect because the word *son* has a short *u* sound rather than a long *o* sound.

24

A is incorrect because the word *ten* has a short *e* sound rather than a long *e* sound.

B is correct because the words *tree* and *key* both have a long *e* sound.

C is incorrect because the word *tie* has a long *i* sound rather than a long *e* sound.

25

A is incorrect because the word *she* has a long *e* sound rather than a long *u* sound.

B is incorrect because the word *fun* has a short *u* sound rather than a long *u* sound.

C is correct because the words *mute* and *few* both have a long *u* sound.

Student Name: _____

Question	Correct Answer	Content Focus	Complexity
1	see below	Character, Setting, Plot: Compare and Contrast	DOK 2
2	A	Sentence (Context) Clues	DOK 2
3A	C	Character, Setting, Plot: Compare and Contrast	DOK 2
3B	D	Character, Setting, Plot: Compare and Contrast/Text Evidence	DOK 2
4	A, E	Antonyms	DOK 2
5	B	Theme	DOK 3
6A	A	Point of View	DOK 2
6B	C	Point of View/Text Evidence	DOK 2
7	D	Connections Within a Text: Cause and Effect	DOK 3
8	B	Sentence (Context) Clues	DOK 2
9	see below	Antonyms	DOK 2
10A	B	Connections Within a Text: Cause and Effect	DOK 3
10B	D	Connections Within a Text: Cause and Effect/Text Evidence	DOK 3
11	D	Figurative Language: Similes	DOK 2
12	C	Point of View	DOK 2
13	B	Figurative Language: Similes	DOK 2
14	A	Theme	DOK 3
15	see below	Free Verse	DOK 1
16	B	Linking Verbs	DOK 1
17	A	Irregular Verbs	DOK 1
18	C	Combining Sentences with Conjunctions to Form Compound Subjects and Predicates	DOK 2
19	D	Apostrophes in Contractions	DOK 1
20	C	Helping Verbs	DOK 1
21	C	Silent Letters	DOK 1

Student Name: _____

Question	Correct Answer	Content Focus	Complexity
22	A	*r*-Controlled Vowel /ûr/	DOK 2
23	B	*r*-Controlled Vowels /ôr/ and /är/	DOK 2
24	A	*r*-Controlled Vowel /îr/	DOK 2
25	C	*r*-Controlled Vowel /âr/	DOK 2

Comprehension 1, 3A, 3B, 5, 6A, 6B, 7, 10A, 10B, 12, 14, 15	/18	%
Vocabulary 2, 4, 8, 9, 11, 13	/12	%
English Language Conventions 16, 17, 18, 19, 20	/5	%
Phonics 21, 22, 23, 24, 25	/5	%
Total Unit 4 Assessment Score	/40	%

1   **2-point response:** Students should compare the thoughts of the two characters at the beginning of the passage. Liam is not worried about trash in the park. After dropping a napkin, Liam asks, "Who cares?" The speaker cares very much that trash hurts the park and thinks that even one action can make a difference. The speaker says, "Think about what the park would look like with twenty napkins on the ground."

9   Students should complete the word web with the following words:
   • boring
   • pale
   • plain

15   Students should mark an X for the following sentences:
   • It does not use rhyme.
   • It does not follow a set rhythm.

Unit 4 Answer Key

Student Name: _____

Narrative Performance Task			
Question	**Answer**	**Complexity**	**Score**
1	B, E	DOK 3	/1
2	see below	DOK 3	/2
3	see below	DOK 3	/2
Story	see below	DOK 4	/4 [P/O] /4 [D/E] /2 [C]
Total Score			**/15**

2 **2-point response:** I learned that animals need plants for food. "Inside a Pond" says that some animals get energy by eating plants. "Under the Ocean" says that some marine animals, like fish and manatees, only eat plants.

3 **2-point response:** This topic is important because some plants and animals can only live on certain "layers" of ponds and oceans. "Inside a Pond" says that a pond skater lives on the top "layer" of the pond. "Under the Ocean" says that plants can only live on the top two "layers" of the ocean. Plants cannot live on the bottom "layer," since no sunlight reaches there.

10-point anchor paper: One day a robin named Harry was flying through the sky. He was on his way to visit the ocean. Harry was thirsty. He wasn't very close to the ocean yet, so he looked for a place to stop for a drink of freshwater. Harry saw a pond near some trees. He flew to the pond.

After landing, Harry saw some pretty flowers, called irises, growing along the pond's edge. He also noticed a plant, called a water lily, growing inside the pond. The water lily's leaves floated on the water. Its roots were under the water.

Harry saw many creatures in the pond. He saw insects, called pond skaters, walking on top of the water. The pond skaters were trying to eat some small insects. Some hungry ducks were eating plant roots. Harry also noticed some tadpoles hiding near the water lily's roots. Some fish were swimming underwater.

The sun was bright, so Harry was able to see to the bottom of the pond. He saw some worms and crayfish on the pond's bottom as he was taking a drink. The worms were eating small parts of plants laying on the pond's muddy bottom. Harry decided it was time to fly on to the ocean.

Harry saw the ocean up ahead. He landed in the sand along the ocean's shore to rest. Harry saw a plant, called seaweed, floating along the shore. He decided to fly over the ocean to look for marine life. Harry saw a couple of seals playing in the ocean. A little later, he noticed a group of sharks swimming together.

Harry knew that the ocean was deep. It was so deep that he couldn't see all of the plants and animals that lived in the ocean. He could only see the plants and animals that lived in the top layer. He wondered what animals lived deep in the ocean as he finished his visit to the ocean.

Unit 4 Rationales

1

See answer key for sample response.

2

A is correct because the word *leaned* means "bent the body in a sloped position" and the word *forward* helps the reader visualize the specific position.

B is incorrect because although the position of the bench may possibly give some context, the word *bench* does not clarify the meaning of the word *leaned*.

C is incorrect because the word *sight* does not help clarify the meaning of the word *leaned*.

D is incorrect because although the downward direction is implied, the word *feet* does not help clarify the meaning of the word *leaned*.

3A

A is incorrect because the characters do not tell the kids to clean up; they do the cleaning themselves.

B is incorrect because there is no mention of finding another park in the selection.

C is correct because the narrator asks Liam if he wants to plan a park clean-up day, and Liam's face lights up in agreement, as he says that they can ask their friends to help work together.

D is incorrect because there is no mention of getting a reward for cleaning up the park.

3B

A is incorrect because although this sentence tells why dropping trash is harmful, it is the narrator's idea but does not tell what Liam thinks about it.

B is incorrect because this sentence tells what the narrator thinks about Liam's action but does not compare what the two friends want to do.

C is incorrect because this sentence tells only about the narrator.

D is correct because this sentence is said by Liam and expresses how he and the narrator both want to do the same thing together.

4

A is correct because the word *neat* is an antonym of the word *messy*.

B is incorrect because the word *useful* is not an antonym of the word *messy*.

C is incorrect because the word *easy* is not an antonym of the word *messy*.

D is incorrect because the word *dirty* is a synonym, not an antonym, of the word *messy*.

E is correct because the word *orderly* is an antonym of the word *messy*.

5

A is incorrect because the focus of this passage is not on friendship but on helping take care of the planet.

B is correct because the most important message in the passage is that even one piece of trash on the ground hurts the planet; we all must do our part to solve the problem.

C is incorrect because the focus of the passage is on helping the planet, not on whether helping others necessarily helps oneself.

D is incorrect because although this statement relates to the dropped napkin in the passage, running out of napkins is not the risk that the passage warns about.

6A

A is correct because the narrator is part of the story's action and talks about him- or herself using words such as *I, me,* and *myself.*

B is incorrect because the narrator talks about him- or herself using words such as *I, me,* and *myself,* which would not be the case if the passage was written from the third-person point of view.

C is incorrect because the point of view of the passage does not change during the action of the passage.

D is incorrect because the point of view of the passage can be clearly identified as first-person, since the narrator talks about him- or herself using words such as *I, me,* and *myself.*

6B

A is incorrect because having events that could take place in real life does not necessarily support the first-person point of view.

B is incorrect because having two characters does not necessarily support the first-person point of view.

C is correct because the narrator is part of the story's action and talks about him- or herself using words such as *I, me,* and *myself.*

D is incorrect because the narrator does use the words *I, me,* and *myself* in dialogue.

7

A is incorrect because bright colors are an effect of Earth waking in springtime.

B is incorrect because green leaves are an effect of Earth waking in springtime.

C is incorrect because people spending time outside is an effect of Earth waking in springtime.

D is correct because the warmer weather is a main cause for Earth waking up and springtime beginning.

8

A is incorrect because the word *world* does not help clarify the meaning of the word *celebrations.*

B is correct because the phrase "or parties" is presented to help clarify the meaning of *celebrations.*

C is incorrect because the word *beginning* does not help clarify the meaning of *celebrations.*

D is incorrect because although spring is the reason for the celebrations, the word *spring* does not help clarify the meaning of the word *celebrations.*

9

The words *boring, pale,* and *plain* are correct because they are all antonyms of the word *colorful.* The words *bold* and *bright* are incorrect because they are synonyms, not antonyms, of the word *colorful.*

10A

A is incorrect because although climbing is exercise, the passage says people climb on the first day of spring for a special reason.

B is correct because the passage says people climb the pyramid on the first day of spring to get closer to the sun and absorb its energy.

C is incorrect because the passage explains a specific reason that people climb the pyramid on the first day of spring, and it is not because of the view below.

D is incorrect because although the pyramid is a very old place, this is not the reason given in the passage for why people climb to the top of the pyramid on the first day of spring.

10B

A is incorrect because the sentence does not state a cause or an effect of people in Mexico wanting to climb to the top of the pyramid on the first day of spring.

B is incorrect because the sentence does not state a cause or an effect of people in Mexico wanting to climb to the top of the pyramid on the first day of spring.

C is incorrect because the sentence describes the action but does not state a cause to support the action.

D is correct because the sentence states the cause of the actions of people in Mexico wanting to climb to the top of the pyramid on the first day of spring.

11

A is incorrect because the passage does not suggest that springtime looks different in different parts of the world.

B is incorrect because although the passage mentions the fact that spring has bright colors, it does not explain why spring has bright colors.

C is incorrect because although the passage mentions the fact that "powdered paint and colored water" are used, comparing the festival's colors to the colors of spring does not show how the festival's colors are made.

D is correct because the statement explains why bright colors are the main focus of the festival that celebrates the arrival of spring.

12

A is incorrect because the speaker talks to something else throughout the poem and remembers what they used to do together.

B is incorrect because the clues in the poem suggest that the speaker is talking to a toy and not to people.

C is correct because the clues in the poem indicate that the speaker is talking to an old toy with paint, wheels, and an engine.

D is incorrect because the clues in the poem suggest that the speaker is talking to a toy and not to a person.

13

A is incorrect because the comparison to a lion does not have to do with humor.

B is correct because the comparison to a lion has to do with how loud the engine is.

C is incorrect because the comparison to a lion does not relate to anger.

D is incorrect because the comparison to a lion does not relate to hunger.

14

A is correct because the speaker discusses a worn-out toy that used to be a favorite.

B is incorrect because although the speaker talks about the past, there is no reference to learning from past mistakes.

C is incorrect because although the speaker refers to an old friend of a sort, this is not done to show that old friends are the best.

D is incorrect because the speaker does not mention any promises in the poem.

15

As a free verse poem, "Together" does not use rhyme or follow a set rhythm. Free verse poems do not have a structure that includes rhythm or rhyme patterns. Telling about the speaker's feelings and describing something from the past are both not specific to free verse poetry. And "Together" does have stanzas; regardless, this characteristic is unrelated to the free verse form.

16

A is incorrect because the plural noun form *boys* should be used here, not a possessive pronoun.

B is correct because the plural verb form *were* agrees with the plural noun *boys*.

C is incorrect because although the verb *going* is correct, there is an error with its helping verb.

D is incorrect because the sentence has a subject-verb agreement error.

17

A is correct because the past-tense verbs *saw* and *said* are the correct verb forms to use to stay consistent with the past tense used throughout the selection.

B is incorrect because the past-tense verbs *saw* and *said* are the correct verb forms to use to stay consistent with the past tense, instead of *seen* and *says*.

C is incorrect because quotation marks are necessary around a direct quotation and because the past-tense verb *saw* is the correct verb form to stay consistent with the past tense.

D is incorrect because the verb form *seen* should be replaced by the past-tense verb *saw*.

18

A is incorrect because a comma is needed before the conjunction that links two independent clauses in a compound sentence.

B is incorrect because a comma is incorrectly placed in the middle of the compound predicate.

C is correct because this choice uses the conjunction *and* to combine the sentences into one sentence with a compound predicate.

D is incorrect because it is a comma splice.

19

A is incorrect because although the apostrophe is placed correctly to form the contraction *weren't*, the past-tense verb *knew* is the correct verb to use to stay consistent with the past tense used throughout the selection.

B is incorrect because the apostrophe is not placed correctly to form the contraction *weren't*.

C is incorrect because the apostrophe is not placed correctly to form the contraction *weren't*.

D is correct because the apostrophe is placed correctly to form the contraction *weren't*.

20

A is incorrect because the helping verb *was* should be replaced by the helping verb *had*.

B is incorrect because the word *mom* should be capitalized only when used as a name, not when preceded by a possessive pronoun.

C is correct because the helping verb *have* does not agree with its subject in tense nor in number in the draft; the word *had* is correct in tense and number.

D is incorrect because the helping verb *have* does not agree with its subject in tense nor in number.

21

A is incorrect because although the word *scent* contains the letter *n*, it does not begin with the /n/ sound.

B is incorrect because the word *crumb* does not begin with the /n/ sound.

C is correct because the words *knock* and *now* begin with the same consonant sound.

22

A is correct because the words *worm* and *dirt* contain the same *r*-controlled vowel sound.

B is incorrect because although the word *right* contains the letter *r*, it does not contain an *r*-controlled vowel sound.

C is incorrect because although the word *dart* contains the same consonant sounds as *dirt*, it does not contain the same *r*-controlled vowel sound.

23

A is incorrect because although the word *far* contains the same consonant sounds as *for*, it does not contain the same *r*-controlled vowel sound.

B is correct because the words *oar* and *for* contain the same *r*-controlled vowel sound.

C is incorrect because the word *hurt* contains a different *r*-controlled vowel sound than the word *for*.

24

A is correct because the words *dear* and *cheer* contain the same *r*-controlled vowel sound.

B is incorrect because the word *chirp* contains a different *r*-controlled vowel sound than the word *cheer*.

C is incorrect because the word *her* contains a different *r*-controlled vowel sound than the word *cheer*.

25

A is incorrect because although the word *fear* is spelled similarly to *wear*, it contains a different *r*-controlled vowel sound.

B is incorrect because although the word *wore* contains the same consonants as *wear*, it contains a different *r*-controlled vowel sound.

C is correct because the words *chair* and *wear* contain the same *r*-controlled vowel sound.

Unit 5 Answer Key

Student Name: _____

Question	Correct Answer	Content Focus	Complexity
1	see below	Connections Within a Text: Sequence	DOK 1
2	D	Text Features: Heads (Subheads)	DOK 2
3	see below	Connections Within a Text: Sequence	DOK 2
4	B	Suffixes *-tion, -ion*	DOK 1
5	A	Text Features: Timelines	DOK 2
6	A	Point of View	DOK 2
7	C	Suffixes *-ful, -less*	DOK 1
8	see below	Multiple-Meaning Words	DOK 2
9	B	Point of View	DOK 3
10	B	Synonyms	DOK 2
11	B	Author's Purpose	DOK 2
12	A, C	Synonyms	DOK 2
13	B	Multiple-Meaning Words	DOK 2
14	D	Text Features: Charts	DOK 2
15A	D	Author's Purpose	DOK 2
15B	B	Author's Purpose/Text Evidence	DOK 2
16	C	Commas in Dates	DOK 1
17	D	Contractions	DOK 1
18	B	Possessive Pronouns	DOK 1
19	A	Capitalization of Proper Nouns	DOK 1
20	C	Pronoun-Verb Agreement	DOK 1
21	B	Diphthongs *ou, ow*	DOK 1
22	A	Diphthongs *oy, oi*	DOK 1
23	C	Variant Vowels /u̇/ and /ü/	DOK 2
24	C	Variant Vowel /ȯ/	DOK 2
25	A	Short Vowel Digraphs /e/, /u/, /i/	DOK 2

Unit 5 Answer Key   Student Name: _____

Comprehension 1, 2, 3, 5, 6, 9, 11, 14, 15A, 15B	/18	%
Vocabulary 4, 7, 8, 10, 12, 13	/12	%
English Language Conventions 16, 17, 18, 19, 20	/5	%
Phonics 21, 22, 23, 24, 25	/5	%
Total Unit 5 Assessment Score	/40	%

1   Students should complete the chart as follows:
   - First... Abigail learns how to read.
   - Next... Abigail marries John Adams.
   - Then... Abigail runs the family farm.
   - Last... Abigail lives in the White House.

3   **2-point response:** Students should include at least two of the following in their answer: Abigail Adams helped First Lady Martha Washington. Abigail Adams became First Lady when John Adams became President of the United States. They lived in the White House. Then the Adams family moved back to Quincy, Massachusetts. Abigail Adams died in 1818.

8   Students should write the numbers of the following two definitions in the word web:
   - 1 — The act of falling, usually because of a bad step
   - 4 — A visit to another place

   Students should then mark an X in the box for definition 4.

Unit 5 Answer Key

Student Name: _____

Informational Performance Task			
Question	Answer	Complexity	Score
1	A, C	DOK 3	/1
2	see below	DOK 3	/2
3	see below	DOK 3	/2
Informational Article	see below	DOK 4	/4 [P/O] /4 [E/E] /2 [C]
Total Score			/15

2 **2-point response:** I learned that people can help other people in an emergency. Paramedics can help people who get sick or hurt by reaching them quickly and then taking them to a hospital. Red Cross volunteers and other workers can help people who are sick or hurt from a disaster.

3 **2-point response:** People who work as paramedics are a team of two people. One drives the ambulance. The other is in back helping the person. Workers in the Red Cross are sometimes in teams, too. Big disasters might need a team of helpers. A person teaching a Red Cross babysitting class or a swim class might work alone.

10-point anchor paper: Paramedics and the American Red Cross make a difference by helping other people. They are alike in some ways. They are different in other ways.

Paramedics main goal is to help hurt or sick people in an emergency. They use ambulances to help take people to a hospital as quickly as possible. The American Red Cross also might help people who need medical care.

The American Red Cross helps people when there are house fires or disasters like hurricanes. They help people get food and housing after these emergencies. Paramedics do not give people food or housing.

The American Red Cross helps people in the armed forces and their families. The Red Cross helps soldiers stay in touch with their families. They also help soldiers' families. Paramedics might help soldiers' families who need quick medical care.

The American Red Cross teaches safety classes like first-aid, swimming and water safety, lifeguarding, and babysitting. Paramedics study and train to learn how to help people, but they do not give classes.

The Red Cross has many volunteers who help others. Adults and children can help. Paramedics are trained workers, not volunteers. Children cannot be paramedics. Both these kinds of workers help people. They are different in some of the ways that they help others.

Unit 5 Rationales

1

Of the events listed, the correct answers reflect the correct sequence of events in Abigail Adams' life. She learned how to read, then married John Adams, then ran the family farm, and then lived in the White House.

2

A is incorrect because the section headings do not focus on reasons Abigail Adams was important.

B is incorrect because the section headings do not focus on people in Abigail Adams' family.

C is incorrect because the section headings do not focus on places where Abigail Adams lived.

D is correct because the sections headings represent different periods in Abigail Adams' life.

3

See answer key for sample response.

4

A is incorrect because the suffix -*ion* does not mean "again."

B is correct because the suffix -*ion* means "the act or process of."

C is incorrect because the suffix -*ion* does not mean "opposite."

D is incorrect because the suffix -*ion* does not mean "more than one."

5

A is correct because the timeline lists four important events in Abigail Adams' life in the order in which they happened.

B is incorrect because the timeline only indicates the times when events happened, not the places where they happened.

C is incorrect because the information provided in the timeline is also provided in the text.

D is incorrect because the timeline does not list any reasons people think Abigail Adams was successful as First Lady.

6

A is correct because the story is told by a narrator who is part of the story.

B is incorrect because the narrator is part of the story.

C is incorrect because although the character of Mom is introduced in the first paragraph, the story is not told by her.

D is incorrect because although the character of Dad is introduced in the first paragraph, the story is not told by him.

7

A is incorrect because the suffix -*ful* does not mean "more than before."

B is incorrect because the suffix -*ful* does not mean "less than afterward."

C is correct because the suffix -*ful* means "full of."

D is incorrect because the suffix -*ful* does not mean "without."

8

"The act of falling, usually because of a bad step" and "A visit to another place" are both definitions of the word *trip*. In the passage, *trip* is used to mean "A visit to another place."

9

A is incorrect because the story is told from the narrator's point of view, so readers do not learn what the narrator's parents want to pack for the trip.

B is correct because the story is told from the narrator's point of view, so readers learn how the narrator feels about preparing for the trip.

C is incorrect because the passage focuses only on the family's camping trip, and there is no mention of what trip might be next.

D is incorrect because the story is told from the narrator's point of view, so readers do not learn much about what the narrator's parents want to do on the trip.

10

A is incorrect because the word *empty* is not a synonym for the word *enormous*.

B is correct because the words *enormous* and *large* are synonyms.

C is incorrect because the word *old* is not a synonym for the word *enormous*.

D is incorrect because the word *soft* is not a synonym for the word *enormous*.

11

A is incorrect because the paragraph does not explain how Habitat was first created.

B is correct because this paragraph explains the ways adults can volunteer with Habitat.

C is incorrect because the paragraph does not explain how Habitat helps people who need better housing.

D is incorrect because the paragraph does not explain ways children can help at Habitat.

12

A is correct because the word *aim* is a synonym for the word *goal*.

B is incorrect because the word *start* is an antonym for the word *goal*.

C is correct because the word *end* is a synonym for the word *goal*.

D is incorrect because the word *beginning* is an antonym for the word *goal*.

E is incorrect because although it may be related in some sports situations, the word *ball* is not a synonym for the word *goal*.

13

A is incorrect because the word *drive* is not used to mean "a trip in a car" in this sentence.

B is correct because the word *drive* is used in this sentence to mean "a project in which people work together to raise money."

C is incorrect because the word *drive* is not used to mean "a need in the body to act in a given way" in this sentence.

D is incorrect because the word *drive* is not used to mean "a strong hit with a club" in this sentence.

14

A is incorrect because the first and second paragraphs share this information, not the chart.

B is incorrect because the chart does not contain this information.

C is incorrect because the first paragraph discusses this information, not the chart.

D is correct because the chart presents the number of people helped in 2017, and it shows three different figures: people helped through improved housing, people helped through training, and people helped in some other way, such as legal advocacy.

15A

A is incorrect because although the author explains what people can do as volunteers, the author does not indicate where to volunteer.

B is incorrect because the author does not show or describe specific types of houses that Habitat has built.

C is incorrect because the author does not explain the history of Habitat in this passage.

D is correct because this sentence and the last sentence of the last paragraph both encourage the reader to volunteer for Habitat.

15B

A is incorrect because although this sentence defines the word *volunteers,* it does not encourage people to volunteer for Habitat.

B is correct because this sentence best expresses the author's reason for writing the passage.

C is incorrect because although this sentence gives details about what Habitat volunteers do, it does not encourage people to volunteer.

D is incorrect because although this sentence gives one possible benefit of working for Habitat, it does not specifically encourage people to volunteer.

16

A is incorrect because the proper noun *Kansas* should be capitalized whenever it appears.

B is incorrect because a comma should not be placed after the name of the month in a date.

C is correct because a comma should be placed between the numerals for the day and the year in a date.

D is incorrect because a comma should not be placed before the name of the month in a date.

17

A is incorrect because the possessive pronoun *her* refers to Earhart, so *his* does not agree in gender.

B is incorrect because the contraction of *did + not* should be written as *didn't.*

C is incorrect because the contraction of *did + not* should be written as *didn't.*

D is correct because the contraction of *did + not* should be written as *didn't.*

18

A is incorrect because both verbs use the same subject (*She*), so a comma should not separate the verb *borrowed* from its subject.

B is correct because the possessive pronoun is referring to Earhart, so the singular possessive pronoun *her* should be used

C is incorrect because the possessive pronoun is referring to Earhart, so the singular possessive pronoun *her* should be used.

D is incorrect because the possessive pronoun is referring to Earhart, so the singular possessive pronoun *her* should be used instead of *my*.

19

A is correct because the word *Ocean* is used here as part of the proper noun *Pacific Ocean*, so both words should be capitalized.

B is incorrect because the word *woman* is spelled correctly in the draft.

C is incorrect because the sentence has an error in capitalization.

D is incorrect because the sentence has an error in capitalization.

20

A is incorrect because the compound subject "she and her plane" refers to two things, so the verb used with it should be the plural *were*.

B is incorrect because the pronoun *she* should be used in the subject of the sentence, instead of the objective case pronoun *her*.

C is correct because the compound subject "she and her plane" refers to two things, so the verb used with it should be the plural *were*.

D is incorrect because the word *Ocean* is used here as part of the proper noun *Pacific Ocean*, so both words should be capitalized, and because the compound subject "she and her plane" refers to two things, so the verb used with it should be the plural *were*.

21

A is incorrect because the word *poor* has an *r*-controlled vowel sound rather than the diphthong and vowel sound in the word *out*.

B is correct because although the word *cow* has a different diphthong spelling than the word *out*, it has the same vowel sound.

C is incorrect because the word *oil* has a different diphthong spelling and vowel sound than the word *out*.

22

A is correct because although the word *choice* has a different diphthong spelling than the word *joy*, it has the same vowel sound.

B is incorrect because although the word *judge* starts with the same consonant sound as the word *joy*, it has a different vowel sound.

C is incorrect because although the word *jaw* starts with the same consonant sound as the word *joy*, it has a different diphthong spelling and vowel sound.

23

A is incorrect because the word *ought* has a different vowel sound than the word *spoon*.

B is incorrect because although the word *spoil* has the same beginning consonant blend as the word *spoon*, it has a different vowel sound.

C is correct because the word *fruit* has the same vowel sound as the word *spoon*.

24

A is incorrect because although the word *could* starts with the same consonant sound as the word *caught*, it has a different vowel sound.

B is incorrect because although the word *catch* starts with the same consonant sound as the word *caught*, it has a different vowel sound.

C is correct because the word *thought* has the same vowel sound as the word *caught*.

25

A is correct because the word *weather* has the same short vowel sound as the word *egg*.

B is incorrect because the word *myth* has a different short vowel sound than the word *egg*.

C is incorrect because the word *touch* has a different short vowel sound than the word *egg*.

Unit 6 Answer Key

Student Name: _____

Question	Correct Answer	Content Focus	Complexity
1A	B	Paragraph Clues	DOK 2
1B	A	Paragraph Clues/Text Evidence	DOK 2
2	A	Connections Within a Text: Problem and Solution	DOK 2
3	see below	Connections Within a Text: Problem and Solution	DOK 2
4	C	Idioms	DOK 2
5	B	Paragraph Clues	DOK 2
6	B	Idioms	DOK 2
7	D	Metaphors	DOK 2
8	B	Elements of a Play	DOK 2
9A	C	Metaphors	DOK 2
9B	D	Metaphors/Text Evidence	DOK 2
10	see below	Theme	DOK 3
11	C	Point of View	DOK 3
12	D	Theme	DOK 3
13	B	Stanza	DOK 2
14	A	Rhyme	DOK 1
15	see below	Point of View	DOK 3
16	B	Prepositions/Prepositional Phrases	DOK 1
17	B	Adjectives Including Articles	DOK 1
18	C	Adjectives That Compare	DOK 1
19	D	Sentence Punctuation	DOK 1
20	C	Apostrophes	DOK 1
21	A	Open and Closed Syllables	DOK 2
22	C	CVCe Syllables	DOK 2
23	B	Consonant + le Syllables	DOK 2
24	B	Vowel Team Syllables	DOK 2
25	C	r-Controlled Vowel Syllables	DOK 2

Comprehension 2, 3, 8, 10, 11, 12, 13, 14, 15	/18	%
Vocabulary 1A, 1B, 4, 5, 6, 7, 9A, 9B	/12	%
English Language Conventions 16, 17, 18, 19, 20	/5	%
Phonics 21, 22, 23, 24, 25	/5	%
Total Unit 6 Assessment Score	/40	%

3   **2-point response:** Students should mention two of the following problems: Ships long ago were not very strong, so there were many shipwrecks. It was hard to see some ships, even though lifesaving crew members looked from the beach and from the lookout tower. People were not able to predict very well when stormy weather was coming.

10   Students should circle the following two sentences:
- Show kindness and you will be rewarded.
- True love can find a way to last.

15   Students should match the following:
- Little mouse—Do not worry.
- Old rat—Be careful.
- Mother—Be careful.
- Robin—Do not worry.

Unit 6 Answer Key   Student Name: _____

Opinion Performance Task			
Question	Answer	Complexity	Score
1	A, D	DOK 3	/1
2	see below	DOK 3	/2
3	see below	DOK 3	/2
Opinion Article	see below	DOK 4	/4 [P/O] /4 [E/E] /2 [C]
Total Score			/15

2 **2-point response:** The picture and caption from "Under the Deep Sea" help me understand what a submarine looks like. I know that it helps protect scientists and other people while they study the living things under the ocean. Riders in a submarine can stay down in the ocean for a long time because there is air to breathe inside. The picture and caption from "Gifts of the Ocean" help me understand one of the gifts that a shellfish makes in the ocean. The pearl from the oyster can be made into jewelry.

3 **2-point response:** People would miss out on many wonderful things if no one explored the oceans. In "Under the Sea," the author tells about people traveling underwater in submarines to take pictures and videos of the living things in the ocean. Scientists study those pictures to learn more about the Earth. "Gifts of the Ocean" said that many ocean plants and animals help people. Some plants can be made into medicines, and others are used for food. People use boats to find these things.

10-point anchor paper: These sources tell about how oceans are important parts of Earth. The underwater world is very large. Scientists have only explored a small part of Earth's oceans. The work of learning about life in the oceans is far from being finished. I think that exploring the oceans by submarine is very useful and will help scientists in the future.

Many years ago people invented submarines to go underwater to look at things. The submarines were built so that people inside could breathe while they were underwater. This helped scientists go to places deep in the ocean, places that boats could not go. They could do experiments to study the living and nonliving things under the ocean. They can help people find ships that sunk or other missing objects.

Not all people may have the chance to travel in a submarine. People decided to take underwater pictures and videos so that people could see what lies under the ocean water. These pictures also helped scientists study the animals and plants that are living in the ocean.

The plants and animals that live in the ocean are helpful to humans. Many are used for food or medicines. Scientists are studying the plants and animals of the ocean. They can get more information about ocean life when they use submarines to help them in their work. Scientists may find even more ways the living things from the ocean can help humans.

The oceans of the Earth are a very special part of our planet. I think that exploring the oceans by using submarines has more benefits than exploring by boats alone.

Unit 6 Rationales

1A

A is incorrect because although a crew is related to a boat, the paragraph indicates that a crew is made of "six people."

B is correct because the paragraph says that a crew is made of "six people."

C is incorrect because the clues in paragraph do not suggest that *crew* is connected to a sport.

D is incorrect because although a crew is related to a kind of job, the paragraph indicates that a crew is made of "six people."

1B

A is correct because these words follow *crew* and best help define it.

B is incorrect because although these words tell where the crew works, the words do not define *crew*.

C is incorrect because although these words tell what the crew does, the words do not define *crew*.

D is incorrect because these words tell about the ships and do not define *crew*.

2

A is correct because this sentence explains the problem ("many shipwrecks") and the solution explored in the passage ("lifesaving stations").

B is incorrect because this sentence does not state a problem or a solution; it describes the lifesaving stations.

C is incorrect because this sentence does not explain the problem being solved; it tells how the lifesaving station crew members did their work, but it makes no mention of shipwrecks.

D is incorrect because this sentence does not state a problem or a solution; it explains a detail about the crew's experience.

3

See answer key for sample response.

4

A is incorrect because, although the crew members were ready to help at night, the idiom "at the drop of a hat" does not suggest this idea.

B is incorrect because the idiom "at the drop of a hat" does not suggest that the crew members waited until they received some kind of signal.

C is correct because the idiom "at the drop of a hat" suggests that the crew members were ready as soon as they were needed.

D is incorrect because the idiom "at the drop of a hat" does not suggest that crew members needed to get equipment or clothing before they were ready.

5

A is incorrect because the word *stations* shows the topic of the paragraph but not the meaning of *remains*.

B is correct because the word *gone* is contrasted (through the conjunction *but*) with *remains*, so its meaning is an antonym.

C is incorrect because the word *summer* does not provide a clue to the meaning of *remains*.

D is incorrect because the word *rescue* is not used in such a way as to establish a clear relationship with the meaning of *remains*.

6

A is incorrect because the idiom "The more, the merrier" is not about the size of a home but rather the size of a group of people.

B is correct because the idiom "The more, the merrier" is used to show that the husband is happy to share his home with his guests.

C is incorrect because the idiom "The more, the merrier" does not mean that the couple rarely has guests.

D is incorrect because the idiom "The more, the merrier" does not mean that the husband wants the guests to stay forever.

7

A is incorrect because no one is in danger in the scene.

B is incorrect because this interpretation relies too literally on the word *sun*.

C is incorrect because Zeus is not feeling embarrassed in the scene.

D is correct because the metaphor gives evidence that the stranger is Zeus and not an ordinary man.

8

A is incorrect because the list of characters in the play is not part of the stage directions.

B is correct because the stage directions show how the characters are feeling and because when the stage directions explain that the stranger's face "is the sun," this is how the husband and wife learn that their guest is Zeus.

C is incorrect because this information is not indicated in the stage directions.

D is incorrect because the dialogue in the play is not part of the stage directions.

9A

A is incorrect because the wife compares Zeus to a star to show how Zeus guides her and her husband, not to explain where Zeus lives.

B is incorrect because the wife compares Zeus to a star to show how Zeus is a source of guidance, not to suggest that he belongs in the sky above.

C is correct because the wife says that Zeus is "the star that guides" them, and then calls Zeus "great one."

D is incorrect because the wife compares Zeus to a star to explain how she and her husband look to Zeus for guidance, not to suggest that he can be dangerous.

9B

A is incorrect because although this sentence tells what the wife is hoping for from Zeus, it does not express that she and her husband follow Zeus.

B is incorrect because although this sentence tells what the wife is hoping for from Zeus, it does not express that she and her husband follow Zeus.

C is incorrect because although this sentence tells what the wife observes about the strangers in their home, even though one of the strangers is actually Zeus, the sentence does not express that she and her husband follow Zeus.

D is correct because the sentence is said after Zeus is revealed as one of the strangers and it expresses directly how the wife and her husband feel about Zeus.

10

The husband and wife showed kindness to the travelers, and Zeus rewarded them well. Also, the couple used their wish to stay together for the rest of their lives. The other theme statements are not supported by the details in the play.

11

A is incorrect because Zeus could still travel to the village with a companion if the play were told from his point of view.

B is incorrect because Zeus could still hide his identity from other characters in the play, so the villagers would still not know the stranger is Zeus.

C is correct because the reader would know Zeus is one of the strangers if Zeus were telling the story from his point of view.

D is incorrect because Zeus could still be welcomed by the husband and wife if the story were told from his point of view.

12

A is incorrect because this line has little relation to the poem's message that you must think before you act.

B is incorrect because this line has little relation to the poem's message that you must think before you act.

C is incorrect because, although the mother trying to stop Robin is indirectly related to the theme, this line by itself focuses only on blind obedience and does not explain the poem's message that you must think before you act.

D is correct because this line tells the overall message of the poem that you must think before you act carelessly and regret it.

13

A is incorrect because the stanzas tell about different characters.

B is correct because the stanzas tell about a mouse that does not think before acting and then a robin that does not think before acting.

C is incorrect because the stanzas have very similar endings in which two animals are caught in life-threatening situations because they do not think before they act.

D is incorrect because the settings are different in the stanzas.

14

A is correct because the words *go* and *know* rhyme.

B is incorrect because the words *other* and *boldly* do not rhyme.

C is incorrect because the words *there* and *think* do not rhyme.

D is incorrect because the words *folks* and *everything* do not rhyme.

15

The little mouse and Robin are the ones who get themselves into trouble because they do not think and they are not worried. The old rat and the mother both try to warn them to be careful, but the little mouse and Robin do not listen.

16

A is incorrect because the conjunction *but* is used incorrectly in the sentence and because the word *around* is a more appropriate preposition for the given context than *about*.

B is correct because the word *around* is a more appropriate preposition for the given context.

C is incorrect because *bodies* is the correct spelling of the plural form of *body* and because the word *around* is a more appropriate preposition for the given context than *about*.

D is incorrect because the word *around* is a more appropriate preposition for the given context than *to*.

17

A is incorrect because the word *usually* is incorrectly and because the article *an* should not be used before the noun *web*.

B is correct because the article *an* is used only before a word that begins with a vowel sound.

C is incorrect because the article *an* should not be used before the noun *web* and because the word *save* should instead be the adjective *safe*.

D is incorrect because the article *a* should not be used before the plural noun *leaves*.

18

A is incorrect because the verb *is* should be replaced by the verb *are* to agree with the plural subject *eyes* and because the comparative adjective *better* should be used to compare two things instead of *gooder*.

B is incorrect because the comparative adjective *better* should be used to compare two things instead of *gooder* and because *than* is the correct word used to show a comparison instead of *then*.

C is correct because the comparative adjective *better* should be used to compare two things.

D is incorrect because *huger* is not a correct comparative adjective form.

19

A is incorrect because although the end punctuation is correct for this statement, the first word in the sentence should be capitalized.

B is incorrect because the sentence does not ask a question; it makes a statement and should end with a period.

C is incorrect because the noun *leaf*, not the verb *leave,* is needed in this sentence and because this statement should end with a period.

D is correct because the sentence does not ask a question; it makes a statement.

20

A is incorrect because the word *too* should replace *to* and because *doesn't* is the correct spelling of the contraction.

B is incorrect because a comma is not needed after the word *that* and because *doesn't* is the correct spelling of the contraction.

C is correct because the contraction of *does + not* should be written as *doesn't*.

D is incorrect because the word *spiders* is the correct plural noun form and does not require an apostrophe.

21

A is correct because the word *kitten* has two closed syllables.

B is incorrect because the word *human* has an open first syllable and a closed second syllable.

C is incorrect because the word *lady* has two open syllables.

22

A is incorrect because although the word *music* has a long vowel, it does not have a CVC*e* syllable.

B is incorrect because the word *napkin* does not have a CVC*e* syllable.

C is correct because the word *describe* has a CVC*e* second syllable.

23

A is incorrect because although the word *grateful* has the same ending consonant sound as the word *shuttle,* it does not end with a final stable syllable.

B is correct because the word *mental* ends with the same final stable syllable sound as the word *shuttle.*

C is incorrect because the word *lately* ends with an open syllable rather than a final stable syllable.

24

A is incorrect because it lists two vowels and two consonants that do not form vowel teams together.

B is correct because *oo* and *ea* are the two vowel teams in the word *moonbeam.*

C is incorrect because it lists a consonant and a vowel that do not form a vowel team together, followed by two consonants that do not form a vowel team together.

25

A is incorrect because the word *counter* has the specified *r*-controlled vowel sound in its second syllable rather than its first syllable.

B is incorrect because the word *silver* has the specified *r*-controlled vowel sound in its second syllable rather than its first syllable.

C is correct because the word *turtle* has the same *r*-controlled vowel sound in its first syllable as the word *circus.*